D1202143

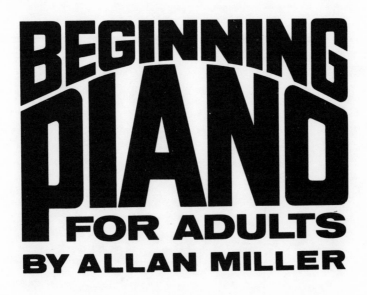

BEGINNING PIANO FOR ADULTS

BY ALLAN MILLER

The Macmillan Company, New York
Collier-Macmillan Ltd., London

I would like to express my thanks to Sara Welles, editor of this book, for her expertise, goodwill and stamina in guiding its preparation.

Copyright © 1970 by Allan Miller
Library of Congress Catalog Card Number 69-10329
Prepared and produced by Rutledge Books, Inc. for
The Macmillan Company
866 Third Avenue, New York, N.Y. 10022
Collier-Macmillan Canada, Ltd., Toronto, Ontario

Printed in the United States of America

FOREWORD

It is possible to learn to play the piano on your own, as an adult.

People have done it before you, successfully. You can, too—if you are determined, tenacious and courageous enough to embark on a difficult but exciting venture.

This book has been written to help you succeed. It goes about teaching you in a way different from methods used for teaching children.

You are starting to play the piano as an adult and must now work at developing muscular coordination and facility you might have developed more easily when you were a child. But there are also some advantages in starting piano this late.

Since you are starting to play because you really want to—you have a growing interest in music and want to be active yourself musically—and not because you have to take lessons, studying the piano is certain to be a more stimulating and satisfying experience for you than for a child. All your past listening experiences can be assimilated into this new learning process. And as you study and practice and learn you will acquire a greater understanding and love of all music—the music you hear at concerts or on records, and the music you play yourself.

This book proposes that you, an adult, do not need to rely upon the rote learning of piano techniques that is the mainstay of instruction for children. For you, learning to play the piano can be far more than a physical exercise—it can be an exciting awakening of your curiosity at the same time. It is the combination of the two—the intellectual and the physical—that is the underlying principle of this book.

For this reason, playing techniques and note reading will be only part of the study to come. You will find as many ideas to think about all through this book as specific instructions, much information that has nothing to do with wrist position and finger dexterity. It is the premise of this book that a broad approach of this sort—moving ahead on several musical fronts at once, looking back into the history of certain techniques and ideas and thinking about their development—is the only way in which an adult can maintain his or her interest and enthusiasm. This enthusiasm will be useful—it will help you to persevere, repeat, practice and learn without a parent or teacher who stands over you with exhortations and threats. And you will emerge a better musician, not just a piano player.

Therefore: do not try to read this book quickly, as you might an article in an encyclopedia or a novel. The information it contains is tightly compressed. The ideas that follow require time to sink in. They cover study that will take you about one year. Each step must be absorbed well before you can move on to the next.

Also you must read the book *at the piano*, practicing as you go, rather than trying to understand it only intellectually. Playing the piano is a physical as well as mental and emotional experience. Just as in any regime of physical exercise, you must begin slowly and build up very gradually.

A reproduction of the complete piano keyboard can be a valuable guide. You can buy it at any store that sells sheet music. If you're ambitious, you can also make one yourself from cardboard.

Take the instructions in small doses. This advice is repeated again and again. Follow it literally.

A word about the organization of this book:

A pupil studying with a teacher can ask questions that cover several aspects of a problem and be shown an answer that covers all of these phases simultaneously. A book must cover one topic at a time. Therefore you will start by finding the notes on the piano before you worry about correct finger position. Also, you will begin learning to play with both hands before you take up the complex problems of rhythmic notation. The order of topics in this book is carefully calculated to get you started in the areas that will enable you actually to play as soon as possible. The organization is as follows:

1. *Learning to read music and to play the notes* on the piano—with any finger, in any manner. This first task teaches you to coordinate what you *see* on the music page with what you *feel* on the piano keyboard. Don't be ashamed to use any and all aids in the beginning.
2. *Learning to use all fingers* in playing these notes, first with either hand, separately, eventually together; here also, through an introduction to intervals, you begin to feel your way along the keyboard.
3. *Rhythm*. Only after you have the feel of the keyboard and don't have to struggle to play notes from the page will you have to face the problem of how long each note is played.
4. *Short pieces*. These are organized by major and minor keys. Now you are playing real music—much of it familiar.

After that, it's just more and more music, including old favorites, the music classics and new material especially composed for you and this book.

Learning to play the piano as an adult should be as much fun as it is work from the very beginning. I believe you can do it. You can learn to play the piano well enough and soon enough to bring you enormous pleasure and satisfaction. I wish you well. I believe in you.

Allan Miller

CONTENTS

INTRODUCTION

The Piano

You'll understand more about the piano and what it can do if you know something of its history.

For several centuries in the history of music, a keyboard instrument held a position of supremacy above all others. In early church music, for example, the organ was the only instrument deemed worthy to accompany the choir and support the service. Outside the church, the harpsichord and clavichord, forerunners of the modern piano, were important solo instruments. They were able to play several notes at once and therefore to fill out the harmony in chamber and orchestral music as no other instrument could.

In the home, the piano has been one of the most popular of all instruments. It is the only one that needs no accompaniment since melodies and chords can be played simultaneously. It is also unsurpassed as accompaniment for solo and group singing.

In times past, when families were dependent upon themselves for entertainment, the keyboard instrument was a social as well as a cultural force. And for the middle and upper classes musical study and proficiency were considered a vital part of one's personal development. One was not considered really educated or cultivated unless he or she played some instrument.

The harpsichord, clavichord and other early keyboard instruments produced sounds from the action of leather or quilled picks that plucked the strings when the keys were struck by the fingers. Each key was connected to two or more sets of strings, depending upon the complexity of the particular instrument. There was no way to vary the attack in order to obtain louder or softer sounds, or sounds of varying tone qualities. Volume or tone quality could be altered only by engaging or disengaging the sets of strings with a foot pedal. Such action was possible, of course, only between large sections of music.

The feature that made the piano different from earlier harpsichords and clavichords was a cleverly conceived mechanical action that enabled hammers to strike the strings with varying strength in order to play both soft and loud notes. Originally, in fact, the piano was called the piano-forte because it could play softly (piano) and loudly (forte).

The piano mechanism transmits the impact from the player's finger on the key to a *hammer* that strikes the string. The string vibrates freely as long as the player keeps the key depressed; this keeps a damper (a felt pad that is wired to the hammer) away from the string. When the key is released, however, the damper falls on the string and stops (dampens) the sound. Hitting the string directly with a hammer instead of plucking it with a preset quill permits the player to exercise more control over the sound of each note, as long as he can control each separate finger. The hammer action was first used in Germany and further developed in England toward the end of the 18th century.

The first pianos had sounding boards of wood; they could therefore sustain only minimal tension in the strings without buckling, and only light striking force by the pianist. Even so, the new variations possible in attack and shading, from one note to the next and within a chord, interested composers in the piano immediately.

Among the first to write music for the piano were Muzio Clementi (1752-1832), Franz Joseph Haydn (1732-1809) and Wolfgang Amadeus Mozart (1756-1791). Mozart wished to learn everything he could about pianos, and he spent many hours in the factory of Johann Andreas Stein in Vienna in 1777. Today we play Bach and Handel on the piano mostly, but their music was originally written for harpsichord.

The English piano maker John Broadwood (1732-1812) strengthened the wooden frame to permit greater tension in the strings and to allow the player a more powerful stroke. Ludwig van Beethoven (1770-1827) owned one of the Broadwood instruments and preferred it to the lighter Viennese pianos. Should you ever have a chance in Vienna or elsewhere to play on one of these pianos of the Beethoven period, you will be amazed at the lightness of sound it produces as compared to the enormous volume of sound generated by today's instruments.

The power and brilliance of today's pianos were made possible by the introduction of iron to the sounding board construction. The first cast-iron sounding board (the big, heavy frame to which the pins holding the strings are attached) was made in Boston by Babcock in 1825. This innovation meant that pianos could employ heavier strings without the risk of cracking or buckling the board. The strings could also be pulled tighter, and the hammers could strike them harder.

10

Throughout the 19th century the iron sounding board underwent improvement and change, especially in the firms of Steinway, Bechstein and Chickering. Research and development still go on. In 1967, the Baldwin Piano Company began to make a new model with still brighter, more brilliant tonal capacity than its predecessors.

Most pianos have two pedals. The left pedal shifts the entire hammer action horizontally so that a hammer strikes only two of the three strings producing any particular note (or only one string if two strings are employed). Thus, with left pedaling, softer sounds are produced.

The pedal on the right keeps the dampers away from the strings, even after the keys have been released, thus producing a more resonant, longer-lasting sound. The right is sometimes referred to as the "loud" pedal.

Technically speaking, however, loudness depends upon the strength with which the key is struck. One accumulates *volume* by holding down the right pedal during unremitting playing. The chief function of the sustaining pedal is that of sustaining sound, as its name implies, and to blend one note with the next. The effect is that of a smooth, tied (legato) musical line, instead of the succession of percussive sounds which are natural to the piano. Using this pedal properly requires a sophisticated co-ordination of finger, foot and ear.

Many pianos have a mysterious third pedal between the other two. This raises the damper from a single note. As the piano is played and notes come and go, this one sound rings through resonantly as long as the pedal is depressed. It is a very special and rarely used effect. It has been remarked that it was only put there to separate the left pedal from the right.

Here are a few vital statistics about the modern piano. Standard pianos have 88 keys (52 white and 36 black). Pianos used in concert halls are called grand pianos and the word "grand" here literally means "large," but also signifies any piano with horizontal sounding board.

Early pianos were harpsichord size, about five feet long. As the sounding boards were strengthened and enlarged, the piano began to assume its present harplike shape. Some pianos today are nine feet long.

Upright pianos have vertical sounding boards. Uprights require less floor space than grands, which accounts for much of the popularity they once enjoyed. A still more compact piano features a shorter keyboard and a still smaller case than the upright. This is the spinet. Originally a spinet was a type of harpsichord, but the modern spinet piano evolved to meet the need for space in cramped city apartments.

And now that the instrument has been introduced to you, it is time to introduce yourself to the piano. You are ready to learn to play.

ONE

First Days at the Piano: Reading Notes

It is always difficult to learn a new physical skill as an adult. Starting a skill that is usually begun in childhood can be embarrassing, especially if there is a youngster in the family who has already achieved a certain degree of proficiency at it. For while a child accepts his beginning lack of skill cheerfully, quite unaware of the awesome gap that separates him from Vladimir Horowitz, you as an adult are likely to consider your beginning inability with despair. Your first sessions at the piano may be fearful ones. You will be afraid of not succeeding, of making a fool of yourself.

It is important to get rid of this fear at the outset, to determine not to be discouraged by the beginner's difficulties. Of course learning to play the piano is a slow process. But you can be sure that you will progress if you keep working at it, and if you don't freeze with fear of failure or humiliation.

From the very beginning each small improvement can bring you pleasure and satisfaction: don't expect too much of yourself and remain confident that your goal is not impossible. You will already be making music in the process.

HOW TO PRACTICE

To practice in private would be ideal. In most households, however, privacy is rare or nonexistent, and the piano is likely to be located in the center of the household, probably in the living room. You cannot pick up the piano and carry it to some quiet place. So you must try to find a time when you can command some degree of calm and peace. Try to gauge the times of day that are most free in your home from telephone and television. Everyone will pick a different hour—early, before work perhaps, or late at night. There are periods in each day when households settle down, when one activity has ended and the next not yet begun. Use these times for your practice.

In the beginning, practicing should be done in very short periods—only ten minutes or so. Go away from the piano after each session, to clear your mind and to let the confusing new ideas settle down inside your head. You must learn to judge when you need to concentrate harder to accomplish a particular task and when you need a change of mental scenery.

During the first week be sure to put in at least three short "lessons" every day. If you skip a day at the outset, you will need three days to recover your momentum. Trying to make up for a missed day by doubling your efforts the next will not work. You cannot cram. Your progress will only be enjoyable if you practice consistently every day.

Once you begin to build up a repertory of small skills, extend the length of time you spend at the keyboard. You will find that this comes naturally since you will not become tired and confused quite so easily. By the end of the first month you should be practicing an uninterrupted half hour each day—including weekends.

When you reach a certain point you will want to play for your own fun those things you have studied. Or you may want to show your family or friends how you are getting along. This is fine—after all, it is why you began to study in the first place. But keep the half hour of concentrated practice time separate. Do not count time spent at the piano which is not part of your home lesson.

The hardest judgment to make when you have no teacher is when to leave one task and go on to the next. Let us approach it this way: learning to play the piano is cumulative in one sense—there are things to absorb before you will be able to understand or perform new material. But since you must move ahead on many fronts, it is not necessary to develop each skill perfectly before you attempt to master the next. You will not be able to read notes perfectly before you learn to use all fingers. And you will still want to practice hearing and playing intervals when you begin to study rhythm. The main thing to remember is to keep coming back to tasks you left. Each practice session should begin with old business before you go on with the new. A few minutes on early material helps to consolidate and polish if you return to it each day.

The amount of time you spend on each subject and the point at which you move on is up to you. But as an adult you will surely know what needs attention and what is fairly well accomplished. You may be doubtful at the outset. But as you cover more and more ground, this will become more apparent to you.

When you sit at the piano, sit midpoint at the keyboard. Adjust your chair or cushion so that you sit high enough to permit your hands to reach the keys easily. The forearms should be roughly parallel to the floor.

Finger techniques are difficult to perfect. We are not concerned with them here. We simply want to get you started playing immediately; we will deal with technique in a later chapter. For now, find a natural, comfortable position for the whole hand, with the fingers curved naturally.

If you were studying almost any other instrument, technique now would be crucial. It requires many hours simply to learn how to draw the bow across the violin string or produce a sound on a wind or brass instrument. But the piano, if correctly tuned, will give you an adequate sound from the very beginning. So you have that hurdle already behind you before you even begin.

Your first task is learning which notes to play. You will learn to read music, that is, learn to translate the markings on the written page of music into finger movements—to strike the correct piano keys.

Looking at the 88 keys on the standard keyboard—52 white and 36 black—notice that the black keys alternate in groups of two and three, and store this fact for later use.

Each of the white keys is designated by a letter of the alphabet, namely, A, B, C, D, E, F and G. The black and white key arrangement appears on your piano keyboard as indicated in this diagram:

The reason for repeating letters after only seven notes is that we are using only seven basic sounds, or notes. Since the sounds are repeated, so, naturally, are their letter symbols.

All notes possessing the same letter designation, or name, resemble each other in sound. All A's sound similar, for example. They appear different in sound only because they are "higher," or "lower."

Perversely, perhaps, though there are only seven different sounds, they are referred to in groups of *eight,* and each group of eight white keys— from one A through the next A, for example, either to right or left—is called an octave. The name comes from the Latin *octem,* meaning eight. On the standard keyboard there are seven octaves plus two extra notes.

This talk of seven notes being eight may be confusing, but in counting we call the first note, one. The seventh note after that is number eight.

For now, notice the uniformity of the keyboard arrangement. Notice, for example, how each A note is in the same position in each octave; that is, it is always between the second and third black keys in the octave's group of three blacks. This uniformity of positioning applies to all notes in all octaves.

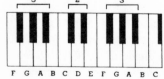

NOTATION

After about a thousand years of gradual development, a standard system of indicating notes on paper was devised. It makes use of parallel rows of five lines, called a *staff*. Each line, and each space between the lines, counts for what is now a different white key on the piano:

The sign 𝄞 at the beginning of the staff is called a *clef* (after the French word for "key") and tells the musician the name of one of the notes, so he can identify the others by their distance from it. The following clef, used by all high instruments (including the upper half of the piano, which is played by the right hand), is called the G clef because the line for G is encircled by part of the clef.

G clef   G   C

The clef itself was originally drawn more like a G: 𝄞𝄞𝄞𝄞
It is also known as the *treble* (for high) clef.

Another clef, or key, designates notes played by low instruments (and the left hand of the pianist). This is the F clef, so called because it has two dots, remnants of the two lines of the F: 𝄢𝄢𝄢𝄢

The dots define the note F below C. It is also called the bass clef.

Put them together, leaving space for one missing line in the middle—a line we will put in for C—and you have the two-staff system used for all piano notation.

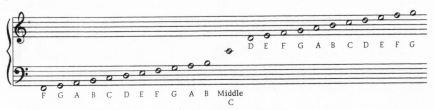

That C in the middle of the two-staff system of written music is called Middle C and is also found in the middle of the piano keyboard—that is, 24 white keys from the left of an 88-key piano:

On a five-line staff, middle C is notated as  or 𝄢

Instead of drawing a line the length of the staff, we make a short line only for that note. This short line is called a *ledger line* and is used to indicate all notes above and below any five-line staff.

F E D C B A etc.

The first space below the staff is F. The next line is the first ledger line, E. The space below that is D, and so on, as far down as is necessary.

Here are ledger lines above the staff, and a G clef staff with ledger notes below and above.

C D E F G etc.   C B A G etc.   A B C D E etc.

You must learn to find a note on the piano after the shortest glance at the page of music. Eventually you should be able to do this without looking at your hands. The fingers must feel what the eyes see. If you have to count the staff lines or spaces for each individual note, you will never read and play even a single line of music fluently. You have to grasp the total picture by the pattern it presents. You are used to this process in other areas. For example, some clocks have no numbers because we are used to telling time by the shape made by the two hands.

Now let us "read" some notes at the piano. Play each of the following notes several times. Play them with each hand. Use any finger on either hand. Sing each note with the letter name as you play it.

A F C E B G F D   A G C E G A B F D A E

In the beginning, work in short sessions throughout the day, with frequent breaks, because the figuring and pondering and checking will easily tire and confuse you. You can practice identifying notes at any time of the day, even away from the piano, by making flash cards or by looking at any page of music to see how long it takes to recognize the notes. Eventually when you see a printed note you will instinctively "feel" the key in your finger. Ultimately you will hear the sound in your mind.

Singing each note, and pronouncing its letter name—A, B, C, D, E and so on—will help to develop this capacity.

The ability to hear music while looking at it on the page is a mystery to most people who do not play an instrument or sing. They can easily visualize colors or shapes with their eyes closed, but hearing music in silence seems impossible. You will discover that this ability can be learned and that your overall musicianship and enjoyment (playing and listening) will improve more rapidly because of it.

BLACK KEYS

So far I have identified and discussed only white keys. Now for the black

16

ones. Each black key has a letter name, borrowed from the white key next to it. This seemingly complex matter is easily explained:

If you move from a white key to the black key to the *right* (toward higher-sounding notes), the black key is called a sharp and is notated (written) on the staff with the symbol ♯. For example, consider an F (white key), indicated on the staff below. The black key to its right on the keyboard is notated on the music as F-sharp.

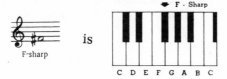

However, if you move from a white key to the *left* (toward lower-sounding notes), the black key is called a flat and is notated on the staff with the symbol ♭.

Now consider a G (white key), indicated on the staff below. The black key to its left on the keyboard is notated on the music as G-flat.

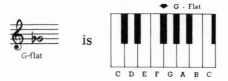

The same black key is used to play both F-sharp and G-flat.

Thus, any black key that is between two white keys can receive either of two letter names (but never simultaneously), depending upon notation. C-sharp, for another example, is the same note as D-flat.

The choice of the composer depends upon the key in which he has written the music. Again, however, you must wait for a fuller explanation of this meaning of the black notes. Moving ahead with basics is the important thing now. Here are some more notes to play, both black and white.

TWO

Intervals

Now that you have made a start, you are going to combine learning the names of the notes on the page, and their position on the keyboard, with the ability to recognize their sound in your ear.

This combination will speed up the process of note identification. Your fingers will also become more familiar with their way around the keyboard.

The first thing we consider is intervals. An interval is the distance from one note to another.

INTERVALS

A melody is made up of notes in sequence. If the notes of a melody are adjacent to each other on the piano—as C and D, for instance—we say the melody moves by steps.

If notes making up a melody are not adjacent—that is, if there are gaps of several lines and spaces (and keys) between them—we say the melody moves by skips, or *intervals*.

You can combine practice in reading and identifying notes with the learning of intervals. There is value in being able to do both simultaneously.

Had you studied the piano as a child you probably would have thought very little about intervals. Your ear probably would have learned to distinguish them on its own over a long period of time.

Because you have waited until adulthood to learn and are now teaching yourself with this book, you can be consciously aware of the structure of intervals. The process of reading notes and hearing the distance, or *interval*, between them can speed up your learning and make it more interesting.

The smallest interval is called a half-step. A half-step is the distance, up or down, from any note to the note next to it, white or black.

From C to C-sharp (written C♯) is a half-step.

Find C and C-sharp (C♯) on the piano. Then sing the two notes, actually pronouncing "C" and "C-sharp," and listen carefully for the difference between them.

From G to G-flat (G♭) is a half-step. Play and sing them.

From E to F is a half-step.

From C to B is a half-step.

If you start from C, count that as number one and move by half-steps up to the next C. You will count 12 half-steps. Play these slowly. Try to sing them as you do, verbalizing with the letter names C, D, E. Then try to sing three or four half-steps in a row, using the piano only to supply the starting note. Use the piano once more to check the last note you sing.

Don't be discouraged if you cannot sing the notes accurately at first. Few beginners ever manage this correctly. Keep at it, though. This kind of ear training is as important as practicing the piano itself. You will progress faster as a pianist if you develop your ear to act as a guide for your fingers. The best, and perhaps the only, way to train your ear is to sing. For then your brain is constructing the intervals and finding the pitches. This will become easier as you read more and more music.

The remainder of this chapter will introduce a number of intervals. Practice a few intervals at a time. Don't try to absorb what is here all at once.

It may take as much as several months practicing them before you become skilled at singing all of them well and recognizing them quickly when you hear them.

This does not mean you have to remain with this chapter, going over these same intervals again and again, without respite. Move on. But always come back to these pages. Use them as practice and reference material as you approach more difficult music and musical ideas.

The study of intervals is a continuous one and should never be set aside. Good musicians never stop practicing intervals. Some musicians carry an A tuning fork wherever they go and use it to sound a starting note either for singing aloud or imagining notes and scales and intervals. You can buy a tuning fork in any music supply shop.

Conductors often begin the study of a score by "warming up" their musical sense or "ear" with exercises using the tuning fork.

Aside from the fact that a tuning fork is always true, you can sound an A in the noisiest surroundings—on a commuter train, say, or in a busy home. You don't have to rap it against a table or a pane of glass. Simply tap it with your fingernail and press its base against the bone behind your ear or against your tooth.

One day you may forget to bring your tuning fork with you and discover that you can hear the A just by imagining the sound of the fork in your empty hand—just as you have heard it hundreds of times before.

WHOLE STEP INTERVALS

It is easy to see what a whole step and a half-step are if you look once again at the piano keyboard:

A whole step obviously is made up of two half-steps. (This measurement is also called a *major second*. The explanation of the term "major" will follow later.)

Play each of the following examples. Sing always C, D, E and so forth, duplicating the piano notes as accurately as you can with your voice. Here are some whole steps. Play and sing each example.

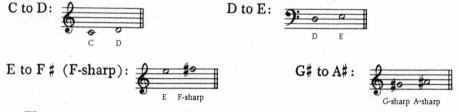

There are many names of intervals, depending upon the distance between the notes. Sometimes an interval is called minor and sometimes major. The terms can be confusing. "Minor" as used here literally means a smaller interval than "major." For example, the next largest interval after a whole step is called a "third," but there are two kinds of thirds—and the minor third is smaller than the major third. A minor third is the distance of a step-and-a-half, or three half-steps.

From C to E♭ is a minor third.

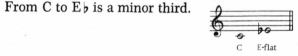

And from F♯ (F-sharp) to A is a minor third.

However, a major third is the distance of two whole steps (or four half-steps.

From C to E is a major third.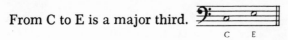

And from C to A♭ is a major third.

The next-largest interval is the fourth—the distance of two whole steps and one half-step.

From C to F is a fourth.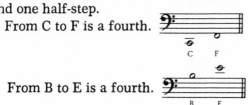

From B to E is a fourth.

You have now learned thirds and fourths. If you have ever played the guitar, you probably noticed that it is tuned to 4ths and 3rds:

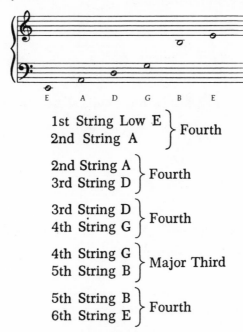

| 1st String Low E | Fourth |
| 2nd String A | |

| 2nd String A | Fourth |
| 3rd String D | |

| 3rd String D | Fourth |
| 4th String G | |

| 4th String G | Major Third |
| 5th String B | |

| 5th String B | Fourth |
| 6th String E | |

An augmented fourth is the distance of three whole steps. Therefore it is also called a tritone—three tones. It is the distance of a fourth increased by one half-step. It is very hard to sing, but try.

From C to F♯ is an augmented fourth.

From F to B is an augmented fourth.

The fifth is the distance of a major third plus a minor third.

From C to G is a fifth.

From B♭ to F is a fifth.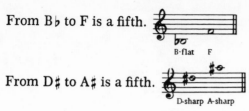

B-flat   F

From D♯ to A♯ is a fifth.

D-sharp A-sharp

The strings of a violin are tuned to fifths: G-D-A-E. The viola is tuned the same way: C-G-D-A; and so is the cello: C-G-D-A, but an octave lower than the viola.

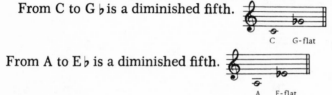

Violin: G   D   A   E   Viola: C   G   D   A   Cello: C   G   D   A

A diminished fifth is a fifth minus one half-step. On the piano it is the same as an augmented fourth but it is notated differently.

From C to G♭ is a diminished fifth.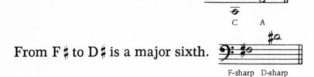

C   G-flat

From A to E♭ is a diminished fifth.

A   E-flat

The next interval to learn is the minor sixth—the distance of a fifth plus a half-step.

From A to F is a minor sixth.

A   F

From C to A♭ is a minor sixth.

C   A-flat

The major sixth is the distance of a fifth and a whole step.
From C to A is a major sixth.

C   A

From F♯ to D♯ is a major sixth.

F-sharp D-sharp

The minor seventh is the distance of a fifth and a minor third.
From C to B♭ is a minor seventh.

C   B-flat

The major seventh is the distance of a fifth and a major third.
From C to B is a major seventh.

C   B

A diminished seventh is a minor seventh shortened at either end by the distance of one half-step. (On the piano it is the same as a major sixth.)

From B to A♭ is a diminished seventh.

From F♯ to E♭ is a diminished seventh.

An octave is the distance from one note to its repetition, higher or lower; that is, a fifth plus a fourth away—C to C, G to G, A♯ to A♯, etc.

There are also names for intervals beyond the octave, as follows:
A minor ninth is the distance of an octave plus one half-step.

A major ninth is the distance of an octave plus a whole step.

A minor tenth is the distance of an octave plus a minor third.

A major tenth is the distance of an octave plus a major third.

An eleventh is the distance of an octave plus a fourth.

A twelfth is the distance of an octave plus a fifth.

I hope you practiced these intervals in small doses. It is hard work, but keep at it, a little each day, even as you move on to later chapters. It will be a great help to your ear and also teaches you to read notes easily.

Before taking up intervals, I spoke of melodies which move by steps. A step, you will recall, is the term for notes that are adjacent to one another. The commonest example of music in a long series of steps is the scale.

All melodies, whether the notes appear in intervals (skips) or in steps, derive from a scale. The scale is one of the fundamental tools of the composer, and as a pianist you will need to understand it fully.

Scales are the subject of our next chapter, and with them you will be able to play real tunes, not just notes.

THREE

First Tunes—Beginning Scales

What is a scale?

A scale is a series of notes, played in order, beginning and ending on a certain key note. This key note is called a fundamental note, and also a *tonic*, from the word "tone." The tonic always imposes its own name on the scale it begins. For example, the major scale shown below begins with C and is therefore known as the scale of C major. The major scale beginning with D would be called D major. Here is the scale of C major, to play and sing:

This scale was derived from an intriguing natural phenomenon that you might like to know about. When you play a fundamental note, such as C, it actually produces a complex group of tones made of the C, plus additional sounds that are heard simultaneously, though only faintly. These are higher tones and are called overtones. Every fundamental tone has its overtones. For example, here are the overtones produced by C below the bass staff. Play them in ascending order:

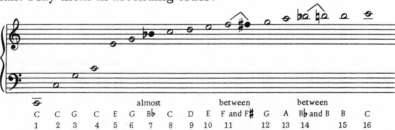

Just playing the low C alone produces all these other higher notes. It requires careful dissection of the whole sound body to distinguish them. The ear of a trained musician can hear many overtones produced by sounding a single note.

The source of overtones is fascinating:

A sound is produced by a vibrating medium. The medium can be the reed of an oboe activating the column of air inside the instrument. It can be a trumpeter's lips on his mouthpiece, also activating a column of air. It can be the strings of a piano.

The string or air medium vibrates *in several motions simultaneously*. For example, over its whole length the piano string vibrates as a unit moving up and down in a bowing motion:

At the same time, the string vibrates in halves of its length. The halves move twice as fast as the whole, producing higher sounds:

While it is vibrating as a whole and in halves, it also vibrates in thirds. These still shorter string segments, moving still faster, produce still higher sounds:

And so on and on.

The basic sound that is heard comes from the vibration as a unit:

But all of the other sounds are present in varying degrees and they could be diagrammed this way:

The quality or "color" of the sound, also called timbre, is determined by the relative strengths of these variously vibrating portions making the overtones; the overtones help to give instruments their distinctive sounds. We distinguish a piano note from the same note on a trumpet partly because the piano produces more of certain overtones than a trumpet does.

25

The trumpet in turn has its own patterns of overtone strengths.

When you played the note C below the bass staff on the piano earlier, it vibrated the C string along the whole, the halves, thirds, fourths and so on, producing all the notes. Here they are again:

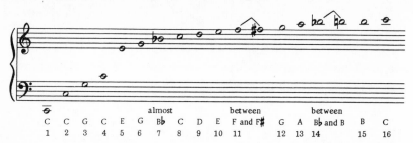

						almost				between			between		
C	C	G	C	E	G	B♭	C	D	E	F and F♯	G	A	B♭ and B	B	C
1	2	3	4	5	6	7	8	9	10	11	12	13	14	15	16

Notice now that the first six notes—C C G C E G—contain three Cs, two Gs and one E. When you play them simultaneously, they form a *chord* which is surely a familiar sound. This is the chord of C major, with the notes C, E and G positioned close together.

Chord (of C major)

The rest of the notes put in consecutive order produce the series of notes known as a scale—the scale of C major:

C D E F G A B C

Actually the scales of western music contain notes that are slightly modified from the true pitch of the original overtones. This allows us to build scales in which all half-steps are the same distance apart. (For further explanations of this complex question, you might want to refer to the "Dictionaries" in the Bibliography.)

Play these notes in ascending and descending order, slowly. Sing each note after you play it. Use any fingers you choose. Play first with one hand, then with the other. This scale of eight notes spans the distance of an octave, from one C to the next.

FORMING THE SCALE

Each note in the scale is located at a certain standard "interval" from the starting or main note—the tonic note of C. Let us see how this scale is formed in terms of steps:

Notice the following:

From C to D is a whole step.
From D to E is a whole step.
From E to F is a *half*-step.

From F to G is a whole step.
From G to A is a whole step.
From A to B is a whole-step.
From B to C is a *half*-step.

This scale is called a *major* scale. A major scale is so named because the first three notes cover the distance of a major third. Any major scale

26

contains a certain sequence of whole steps and half-steps, with the half-steps in the same order, no matter which note the scale begins on. The name of the scale comes from the tonic—the note on which it begins and ends. For example, let us build a scale beginning on the note G:

Play this slowly and sing the intervals.

Note that the seventh note, called the leading tone because it leads by a half-step to the tonic, is here played on a black key, F♯. You know now that the scale of G major has one sharp, F♯.

The scale of D major, you will see next, has two sharps—the same F as in G major, plus one more for the leading tone—C :

In order to preserve the order of whole steps and half-steps, it becomes necessary to lower, or to "flat," the fourth note of the scale. In the scale of F major, a fifth *below* C major, we find one flat—B-flat:

A fifth below F is B♭. It contains the B♭ of the previous scale, F, and adds a new one, E♭:

Later we will learn to play all the scales. Now, however, the task is to become fluent in a few of them, in order to learn to read notes easily.

After all this thinking and singing, using scales and intervals, here are some melodies made up of these musical tools. These are simple melodies based largely on scales, or "stepwise" motion. Later you will play some melodies that use larger intervals—melodies that "skip" around more.

Here is the first part of the melody, "My Country 'Tis of Thee." See how it centers around C. It will sound strange because it is notated without regard to rhythm.

Here it is starting on G:

Here it is starting on A♭:

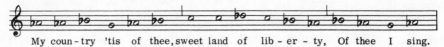

My coun-try 'tis of thee, sweet land of lib - er - ty, Of thee I sing.

The second half of this melody starts on the fifth note of the scale. In C major:

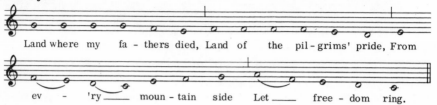

Land where my fa - thers died, Land of the pil - grims' pride, From ev - 'ry__ moun - tain side Let __ free - dom ring.

In G major:

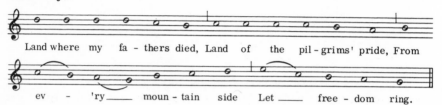

Land where my fa - thers died, Land of the pil - grims' pride, From ev - 'ry__ moun - tain side Let __ free - dom ring.

In A♭ major:

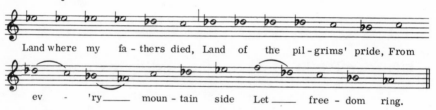

Land where my fa - thers died, Land of the pil - grims' pride, From ev - 'ry__ moun - tain side Let __ free - dom ring.

Now here is the whole melody, without rhythm, in C major:

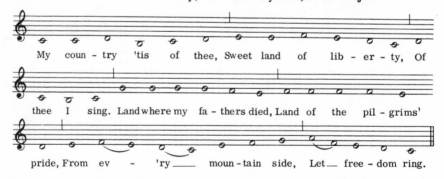

My coun - try 'tis of thee, Sweet land of lib - er - ty, Of thee I sing. Land where my fa - thers died, Land of the pil - grims' pride, From ev - 'ry __ moun - tain side, Let __ free - dom ring.

Every note of the scale is used during the course of this melody. No other note is used but notes in the C major scale.

Notice also that the melody is divided into two clearly delineated sections, or phrases. Each phrase is itself constructed of repeated themes or leading phrases, sometimes called *motives*. The sixth note of the scale is used only once, almost at the end of the melody, on the word "Let." Since it is also the highest note of this melody, it functions as the *climax* and is not repeated. Later when we are able to analyze the rhythmic structure of this very simple tune, we will see that from a rhythmic point of view as well it is carefully put together.

Here is "Twinkle, Twinkle, Little Star" in various keys. This melody uses all but the seventh tone, the leading tone of the scale, but is also clearly in C major because it begins and ends on the tonic C, which is repeated for emphasis—along with the fifth, G. In the overtone series, the note a fifth from the fundamental is the strongest note, next to a repetition of the tonic. Here (again without rhythm) is the melody in C major:

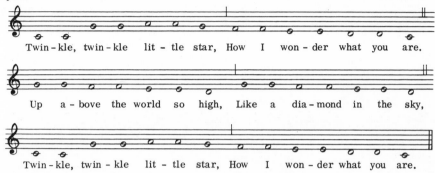

The form of this melody is in three parts. It has a large section or phrase (divided into smaller parts), a middle section or phrase (based on a repeat) and the first large section again. This tripartite A-B-A form is so common in song melodies that it is sometimes called "song form."

Here is the same melody, played in B♭ major:

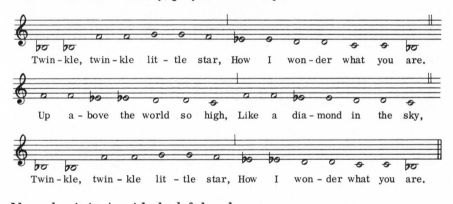

Now play it in A, with the left hand:

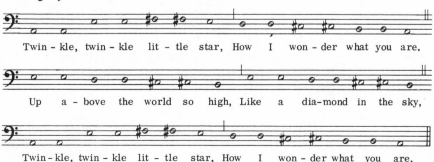

29

A melody need not begin on the tonic note of the scale in which it is written. It will almost always end on it, however. "Mary Had A Little Lamb," written here in three ways—in C, D and E-flat—is a good example:

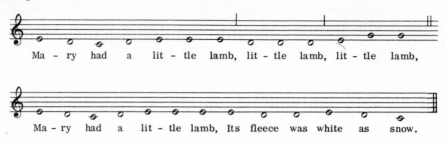

Ma - ry had   a   lit - tle lamb, lit - tle lamb, lit - tle lamb,

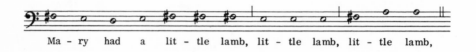

Ma - ry had   a   lit - tle lamb, Its fleece was white as   snow.

Ma - ry had   a   lit - tle lamb, lit - tle lamb, lit - tle lamb,

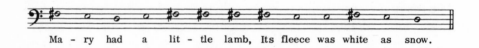

Ma - ry had   a   lit - tle lamb, Its fleece was white as   snow.

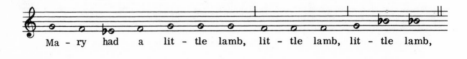

Ma - ry had   a   lit - tle lamb, lit - tle lamb, lit - tle lamb,

Ma - ry had   a   lit - tle lamb, Its fleece was white as   snow.

Now you have been introduced to notation and scales. Though it has involved concentration and hard work at the piano we have not been too taxing on the fingers.

You have already accomplished a good deal. You now know how to translate symbols on the page into sounds on the piano, and you have started to train your ear so that it is more accurate and more attentive.

It is now time to study a third phase—pianistic technique, which you will develop side by side with an ever keener ear and more fluent reading ability.

FOUR

Technique—Posture, Hands, Fingers

Sitting at the piano should never be tiring and should never make you stiff or cramped. After all, sitting at the dinner table never does. You should not have to practice correct posture: there is no technique needed for sitting down—or up. Sitting at the piano should look and feel natural and comfortable.

There is a certain use to be made of the body, though body motion should be kept to a minimum. The source of strength in the fingers and hands is the arms, shoulders and torso. The arms and wrists should be flexible and relaxed in a natural way. What you must ultimately achieve is strength, control, agility and, above all, independence of the fingers.

The wrist must be held evenly at an unchanging angle, naturally elevated from the keyboard. Do not rotate the wrist, or raise or lower it in order to add power or expressiveness to the fingers. Let each finger learn to operate on its own—supported but not governed by the hand and wrist.

THE HAND AT THE PIANO

Bring your right hand to the keyboard. Place all five fingers on any five adjacent white keys. Do not press them as yet (photograph 1).

The fingers should be curved. The weight of your arms and hands should be concentrated in the fingertips. Without moving any of the other fingers, lift the index finger as high as it will go (photograph 2) and allow it to fall through the level of the other fingers until the key is depressed and the note sounds (photograph 3). Do not collapse your wrist or try to help the finger motion with the hand; raise the elbow to get more arm power. The finger should simply fall from the top of its arch through to the bottom of the key in one swift, heavy, smooth motion.

Repeat this movement with each finger.

Now place the left hand in playing position above another five keys.

31

Repeat the motions described above with the fingers of the left hand.

Then do the same with all ten fingers at the keyboard, in any order you choose, making sure to lift each finger high before striking the key. Repeat this exercise with concentration for three or four minutes.

Then do something else for a while. Try singing intervals, perhaps, or something that will employ what you have learned about intervals.

When you return to the piano, repeat this first fingering exercise for several more minutes. Do not permit your curved fingers to "cave in" at the joints under pressure of playing. Also, clip your fingernails so that the fleshy fingertips strike the keys without clicks.

MOVING THE FINGERS IN SUCCESSION

Moving from one finger to another involves a particular pattern for your hands. Try first playing A and B with the third and second fingers of the left hand. To do so easily, place the fingers on white keys with the thumb on middle C.

Now raise the third, or middle, finger. When this finger falls downward to play A, raise all the other fingers simultaneously, including your thumb. Concentrate on the index finger, now poised to play the next note, the B (photograph 4). All the body weight should be concentrated on the third finger playing the A.

Get ready to play B. When you play B with the second finger, raise the third finger simultaneously. Try this several times, very slowly back and forth, A-B, A-B, carefully watching your fingers as you do so. Observe how they perform.

Then do the same with other pairs of fingers. Use the right hand, working until you begin to see some success in making your fingers instinctively pass in midair. Lift, strike. Lift, strike. Lift, strike.

Once again, however, don't overdo things. At first you will be able to repeat these motions profitably only for short periods, ten minutes or so to start. After working on the lift-strike motion for a few days, apply it to more than only two notes at a time. For this, you can return to the scales introduced in Chapter Three. Remember to sing the tones as you play until you can play with such speed that your voice cannot keep up with your fingers.

RIGHT-HAND FINGERING

Here is the fingering for the C major scale, using the right hand:

C	D	E	F	G	A	B	C
1	2	3	1	2	3	4	5
(Thumb)		thumb under					

The numbers you see written on the staff refer to the fingers and thumb of the right hand, the thumb being number one. Notice the use of the thumb. To play a note with it the second time, on the F, you must move it *beneath* your hand. For an instant it will be concealed by your palm.

Start this thumb movement as soon as you have played C. By the time you play E, the thumb should already be in position beneath your palm to play F (photograph 5).   **5**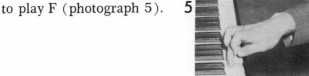

There is good reason for this shift, and perhaps it is already obvious to you. If you do not move the entire hand to the right you will run out of fingers with which to play all the notes indicated on the staff.

Now give it a try. Proceed slowly. This crossing of thumb and hand is not something one generally masters on the first attempt. Check each motion. Advance only when you feel a note has been played correctly. You will need patience. You will have to repeat and repeat. Be your own harshest critic; evaluate yourself with scrupulous honesty. It is likely no one else will; if you can say you are playing with proficiency, move ahead.

If you cannot, carry honesty one painful step farther and practice the lift-stroke exercises again before moving on.

When you have practiced playing from low to high notes for a while, try the process in reverse. Start with the notes at the top, beginning with the fifth finger, and move downward. Cross the third finger *over* the thumb moving from F to E.

LEFT-HAND FINGERING

Now here is the fingering for the left hand:

C	D	E	F	G	A	B	C
5	4	3	2	1	3	2	1
				cross over			

First start with the fifth finger and play to middle C. Then start with the thumb first and play from high to low.

Remember always that you must feel your body and arm weight firmly implanted at the end of the depressed finger, not in the arms or hands. Moving from one note to the next with simultaneous lift-strike movements means instantaneous transfer of weight from one finger to another. Remember also to include your ear in your playing. Listen. Sing each note

33

before you play it. Test the accuracy of your listening and singing by whether the note you sang matches the correct one struck by the piano.

After practicing the whole scale as a unit for a few days, it will be time to start some exercises which alternate the adjacent notes you play. Include the following in your daily practice. Try making up others yourself. Play each one backward as well as forward.

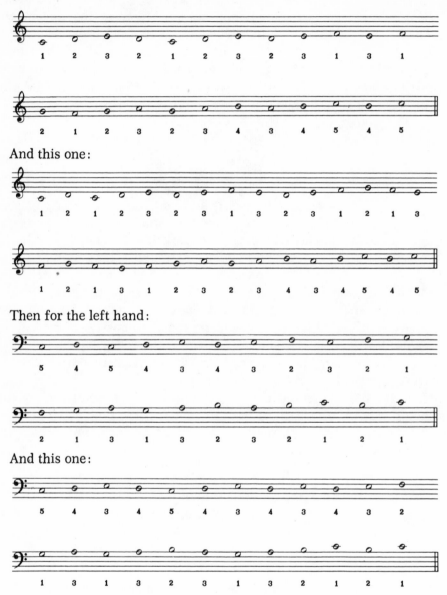

And this one:

Then for the left hand:

And this one:

By now you should be developing some skill at moving from finger to finger. I hope you are beginning to feel more at home with the piano as a result of this, and that you take pride in your accomplishments to date. You have only begun, but your beginning is significant. You can read notes and find tunes on the keyboard.

Let us return now to the tunes we picked out in Chapter Three. Play them now with more precise fingering and feeling. First try "Mary Had A Little Lamb," starting with the left hand:

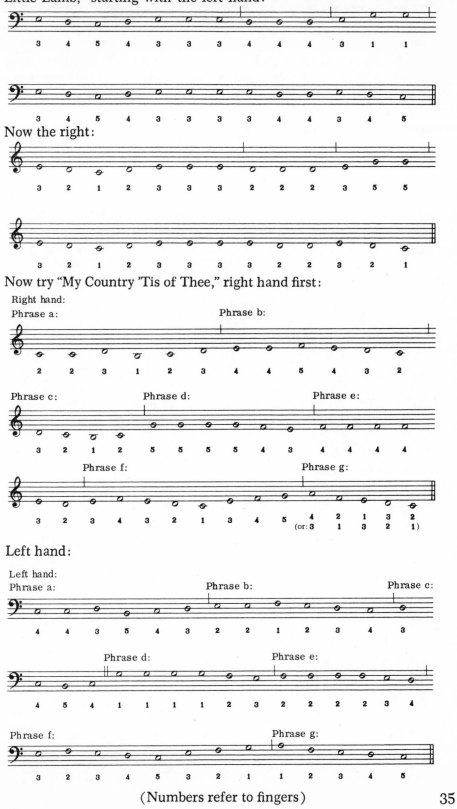

Now the right:

Now try "My Country 'Tis of Thee," right hand first:

Right hand:
Phrase a: Phrase b:

Phrase c: Phrase d: Phrase e:

Phrase f: Phrase g:

Left hand:

Left hand:
Phrase a: Phrase b: Phrase c:

Phrase d: Phrase e:

Phrase f: Phrase g:

(Numbers refer to fingers)

By the way, we call the form of this kind of melody *through composed* because there are no sections repeated melodically. Each new line of text is set to a new musical section called a phrase. Phrases d and e have the same melodic shape, though they begin on different notes: one note played four times, the next note one step below and then a note one step below that. This repetition of a pattern on a different pitch level is called a *sequence*. The opening of the famous Fifth Symphony by Beethoven is built on a sequence. Here are the pitches. Each of the two groups of notes consists of three repeated notes plus one note a third below:

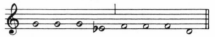

EXPANDING SCALES

The range of a melody is the distance between its lowest and highest notes. So far most of the music we have practiced contains melodies that fall within the range of one octave. All the notes of "Mary Had A Little Lamb" fall within the range of a fifth:

"My Country 'Tis of Thee" has the range of a minor seventh.

"Twinkle, Twinkle, Little Star" has the range of a major sixth:

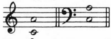

Music composed within ranges greater than one octave requires that you be able to play scales that go beyond one octave, and for that, you must learn additional fingering. This new fingering includes additional crossing of the thumb so that you will be ready to continue the basic fingering in the new octave.

Here is the C major scale in two octaves. First use the right hand; play up and down:

Your hand must move farther to cross from the fourth finger to the thumb than it does from the third finger.

Now, using the left hand, play up and down:

Here are a few exercises involving these crossings:

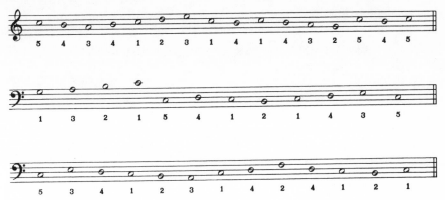

When you feel you can play these crossings fairly easily, practice scales over a range of four octaves, one hand at a time.

You must now start to listen for evenness in your playing. Though played freely, without excess restraint or excess force, each note should sound with the same even quality and the same volume. The best way to practice this is to play each note as softly as possible. You will discover which fingers you cannot control—they will produce sounds that are louder than the rest. Further, the notes will inevitably be played with a lunge, producing an accent. Work toward controlling each finger as much as possible.

Now you should also begin to practice scales evenly in time, say, one note every two seconds. Eventually increase the speed, always maintaining a smooth, even fingering.

All this will take time and patience. Most pianists continue this kind of exercise indefinitely. It requires constant effort to achieve evenness of technique, and maintaining it is as difficult as achieving it. As yet, don't try to play any faster than you can play smoothly. Alternate practice of scales with other exercises—intervals, singing and so on. Work on your weaknesses, but don't torture yourself.

The composer Robert Schumann (1810-1856) devised a contraption for strengthening a weak finger. But it permanently maimed his hand and ended his career as a pianist. So don't try to go too far, too fast.

On the other hand, throughout your study you will always be moving just a little beyond your limit, learning new music and new techniques before earlier ones are perfected. This does not conflict with what was said earlier about evaluating yourself honestly, not pushing ahead until ready. The study of music is a cumulative process, and you cannot skip a step. You can, however, study several steps simultaneously. The trick is to find a balance between dwelling too long on one and rushing carelessly ahead.

When you reach the end of this book, you should still be practicing exercises found in the opening chapters. You should be practicing them at a more advanced level and at faster pace, however.

Some students find their balance by working on something *one* step beyond current material, and one step only. This one-step plan permits them to move ahead so they are not bored and yet prevents them from rushing too fast.

Here is a melody with a range exceeding one octave. The right hand first:

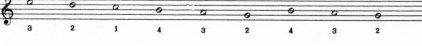

Now the left hand:

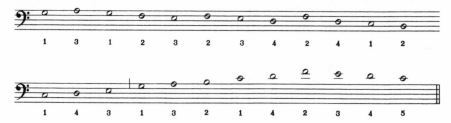

MELODIES WITH SKIPS

Here is "Twinkle, Twinkle, Little Star" again, a melody which uses skips as well as steps, a feature of most music:

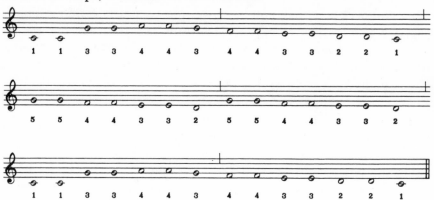

The beginning of the "Star-Spangled Banner" has a wide range, and more skips.

The main phrase of "The First Noël," used for the chorus as well as the verse, is almost completely stepwise:

Left hand:

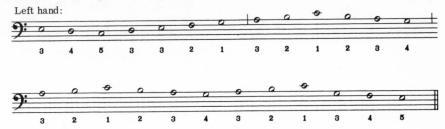

"Silent Night" combines steps and skips fairly equally. Try for fun playing with both hands together. Analyze the form of the melody:

A skip, you will recall, is the distance of more than one note between two notes on the staff or on the piano.

Fingerings for all scales will be discussed soon.

Now that you've learned to play notes and tunes, it is time to learn to play them in time—that is, with *rhythm*.

Rhythm is pattern. Rhythm is timing. Rhythm is what gives music its forward motion—its beat, its bounce.

FIVE

Rhythm

Until now the only written notes you have seen have been simple circles indicating pitch and designating the keys to strike.

These circles are also called whole notes. They are counted for twice as many beats as half notes:

They are counted for four times as many beats as quarter notes:

There are also eighth notes:

And sixteenth notes:

And thirty-second notes:

And even sixty-fourth notes:

The direction of the stem of a note (the vertical line) has no rhythm or pitch significance; it conveys no musical instruction. If the body of the note (the circle) is in the upper half of the staff, the stem is drawn downward:

If the note appears in the lower half of the staff, the stem is drawn upward:

If the body of the note is drawn on the middle line of the staff, you may take your choice, but the stem is usually drawn in the same direction as those around it, for unity's sake. To repeat:

Four quarter notes equal one whole note: ♩ ♩ ♩ ♩ = 𝅝

Two half notes equal one whole note: ♩ ♩ = 𝅝

Two eighth notes equal one quarter note: ♪ ♪ = ♩

Two sixteenth notes equal one eighth note. This can be written on the staff in two ways: ♬ or ♬ equal ♪

Two thirty-second notes and one sixteenth note equal one eighth note. That is, all three are played within the time allowed for the eighth; this is another complexity which will be covered further on. This combination and others employing thirty-seconds and sixteenths can also be written in two ways: 𝅘𝅥𝅲 𝅘𝅥𝅲 𝅘𝅥𝅯 or 𝅘𝅥𝅲𝅘𝅥𝅲𝅘𝅥𝅯 equal ♪

Two eighths, one quarter and one half equal one whole. This is but one of several possible combinations of fractional notes adding up to a whole note. ♪ ♪ ♩ ♩ or ♪♪ ♩ ♩ equal 𝅝

MOVING AHEAD . . .

In most western music rhythm is created by organizing notes into repeated patterns called meters within which some notes are played with more emphasis than others. An example of such a pattern is the waltz rhythm with its distinctive *One*, two, three . . . *One*, two, three beat. These patterns fall into units called measures.

The beginning of each new measure is indicated by a line. The heavy double line means the end of the piece.

If a measure is divided into four equal pulses, or *beats*, then we count 1-2-3-4, 1-2-3-4 and so on.

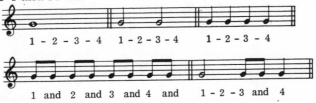

1 - 2 - 3 - 4 1 - 2 - 3 - 4 1 - 2 - 3 - 4

1 and 2 and 3 and 4 and 1 - 2 - 3 and 4

At the beginning of each piece of music, following the clef (𝄞) sign, there is an indication of the way the measure is to be counted; this is called a *time signature*. The top figure tells the number of beats in each measure. The bottom figure indicates the unit or pulse in which the count is to be made; quarter notes, halves, sixteenths, and so on. 𝄴 means, for example, there will be four beats in the measure, each beat to be a quarter note:

1 - 2 - 3 - 4 - 1 - 2 - 3 - 4

$\frac{2}{4}$ means two quarter notes in each measure:

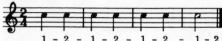

1 - 2 - 1 - 2 - 1 - 2 - 1 - 2

$\frac{2}{8}$ means two eighth notes in a measure:

1 - 2 - 1 - 2 - 1 - 2 - 1 - 2

$\frac{2}{2}$ means two half-note pulses in each measure:

1 - 2 - 1 - 2

$\frac{4}{4}$ is sometimes written as a C:

1 - 2 - 3 - 4 - 1 - 2 - 3 - 4 - 1-2-3-4

$\frac{2}{2}$ is sometimes written as $\mathcal{C}$:

1 - 2 - 1 and 2 - 1 - 2 and 1 - 2

The signatures above divide each measure in multiples of two. We can also divide a measure into three beats, as in the waltz. Quiet breathing, too, is usually a three-part activity—one beat for inhaling, two beats for exhaling.

$\frac{3}{4}$ means three quarter notes in each measure:

1 - 2 - 3 - 1 - 2 - 3 - 1 - 2 - 3

$\frac{3}{8}$ means three eighth notes in each measure:

1 - 2 - 3 - 1 - 2 - 3 - 1 - 2 - 3 - 1 - 2 - 3

$\frac{3}{2}$ means three half notes in each measure:

1 - 2 - 3 - 1 - 2 - 3 - 1 - 2 - 3

$\frac{3}{8}$ seems to be somewhat faster than $\frac{3}{4}$; in $\frac{3}{8}$ a pulse is usually felt only every first beat of the measure:

1 and and   1 and and   1 and and   1 and and

In $\frac{3}{4}$, although the first beat is the strongest, each of the others has an individual beat of its own. This might well be illustrated by comparing two lines of poetry:

Come, friends, let   glad   tid - ings   sound 'round the   realm

Lis - ten my   chil - dren and   you   shall hear

42

In addition to simple binary $\frac{4}{4}$ $\frac{2}{4}$ $\frac{2}{2}$ and simple ternary $\frac{3}{4}$ $\frac{3}{8}$ $\frac{3}{2}$, great use is also made of $\frac{6}{8}$. This is called compound time because it combines binary and ternary. In this combination there are *two* main beats to the measure. Each beat is divided into three eighth notes:

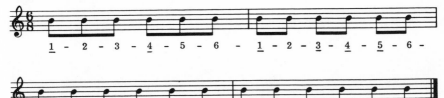

$\frac{6}{8}$ can also be divided into three groups of two eighth notes:

Try counting the beat of the following measures out loud, accenting the first note of each group of three, maintaining a steady cadence. Also, clap. Do so with an accent on the underlined notes. You will notice a strong, pulsing feeling.

Repeat the above often to develop the knack of quickly reading rhythmic notations. Below are some more exercises which will help you further in the quick reading of rhythmic notation.

At this time you might want to get a metronome. This is a clockwork mechanism that marks the exact musical beat with clicks. A metronome is accurate; it will keep a regular pulse without variation, relieving you of this burden when you are first learning and want accuracy. Professional musicians still use metronomes during practice after years of playing.

At the beginning of each exercise set the metronome at the suggested marking for whatever beat is specified. This marking is seen on the written music as the abbreviation mm, meaning metronome marking. It is followed by symbols telling you the setting of the basic pulse. For example:

M.M. $\d = 60$. The half note is set at 60 on the metronome.

M.M. $\d = 108$. The quarter note is set at 108.

If the markings in these exercises seem too fast, slow them down to a point at which you can do the exercise at a steady, regular pace.

In the beginning, clap these rhythms before you play them, counting beats out loud with your voice. The abbreviation cl. stands for "clap," of course.

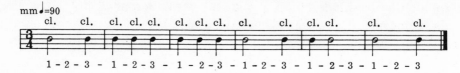

mm ♩=90

1 - 2 - 3 - 1 - 2 - 3 - 1 - 2 - 3 - 1 - 2 - 3 - 1 - 2 - 3 - 1 - 2 - 3

Keep in mind, too, that a musical piece can begin on an *upbeat*. That is, it can open on a light pulse before the *downbeat* at the beginning of the measure.

mm ♩=120

3 - 1 - 2 - 3 - 1 - 2 - 3 - 1 - 2 - 3 - 1 - 2 - 3

It can begin anywhere in the measure:

mm ♪=132

2 - 3 - 1 - 2 - 3 - 1 - 2 - 3 - 1 - 2 - 3 - 1 - 2 - 3

It can also end anywhere in the measure.

mm ♩=80

1 - 2 - 1 - 2 - 1 - 2 - 1 - 2 - 1 - 3 - 1

mm ♪=112

1 - 2 - 3 - 1 - 2 - 3 - 1 - 2 - 3 - 1 - 2 - 3 - 1 - 2 - 3 - 1 - 2 - 3 - 1 - 2

Remember: the heavy double bar drawn vertically from top to bottom of the staff indicates the piece is at an end.

Two other notational marks should now be introduced. Both do a great deal to simplify written music.

One is the tie ⌒ between two notes:

This indicates that the two notes are combined to be played as one note, without interruption. Examples: is counted

```
        clap    clap
         ♩       ♩
        1 - 2   1 - 2
```

With a tie, however, these same two half notes are played as a whole note: is counted

```
          clap
           ○
        1 - 2 - 3 - 4
```

Other examples:

Two quarter notes with a tie now equal a half note, that is:

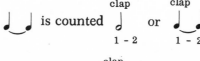

```
              clap           clap
   ♩  ♩         ♩      or      ♩ ♩
  is counted                 1 - 2
              1 - 2
```

In 3/4 time: is counted

```
         clap
          ♩  ♩
        1 - 2 - 3
```

44

In $\frac{3}{8}$ time:  is counted

Sometimes the tie is used from one measure to the next, across the bar line, as follows:

The second notational mark is the dot [•]

The dot adds half the value of the note it follows to that note. Examples:

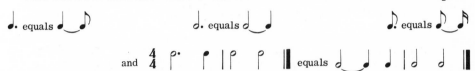

Try these measures with the dot added, clapping every rhythmic change, counting every beat out loud:

Do you recognize "Mary Had A Little Lamb"? Almost exactly the same rhythm is used for "London Bridge."

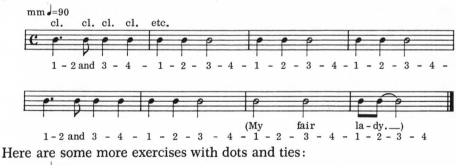

Here are some more exercises with dots and ties:

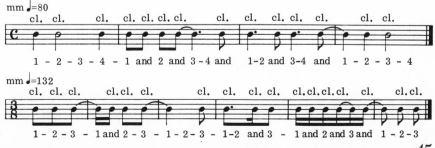

Now, instead of clapping, play the notes slowly with either hand. Continue to count aloud the basic beat of each measure.

Here are some harder exercises:

This is the start of "Alexander's Ragtime Band":

Here is the best-known phrase from Schubert's Unfinished Symphony:

RESTS

Music is never continuous, uninterrupted sound (except in restaurants and elevators). There are often pauses or rests within the music and these are as important as the sounds. As the jazz musicians say, "It's what you don't play that counts." Rests are notated for the same time values as notes:

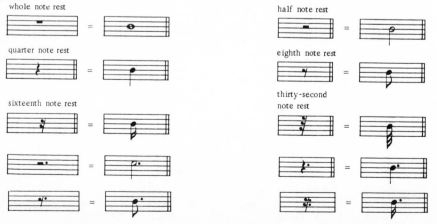

In order to feel the length of the rest we must now listen to the duration of the sounds when we practice rhythmic exercises. Instead of counting the beats of a measure out loud and clapping the changing notes, count silently. Instead of using numbers, imagine each note as "ta." Mentally hold each ta for the number of beats indicated by the note in the written music. A whole note is a long ta-a-a-a-a. A quarter note is a shorter ta-a-a.

When there is a rest, keep silent:

Here are exercises combining rests, ties and dots:

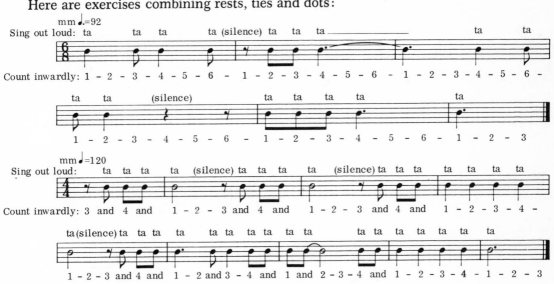

This last one is "When the Saints Go Marching In." Try it:

Now you are ready to try more tunes. You probably already know how to sing some of them. Fingering instructions will be provided. Treat them as exercises and be rigorous about mastering them—*in time*.

If another member of your family or a friend can play the guitar, he can accompany you with the chords indicated. But don't invite someone else to practice with you unless you feel comfortable with him. Learn the music on your own. Be confident enough and proud enough not to make someone else wait for you while you stumble repeatedly over the same passage.

There is no half way. You either can play without error or you can't. You should know the music so well that you can listen to your accompanist's playing as well as to your own and be sure of your judgment of tempo (speed), dynamics (loud and soft) and ensemble (playing accurately together). To help you in these areas, try singing as you play.

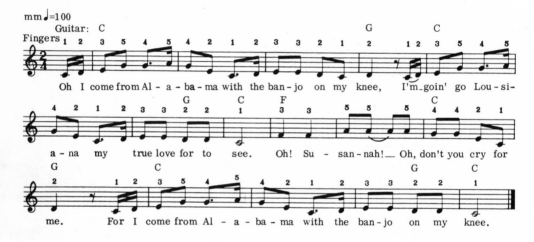

Brahms' Lullaby

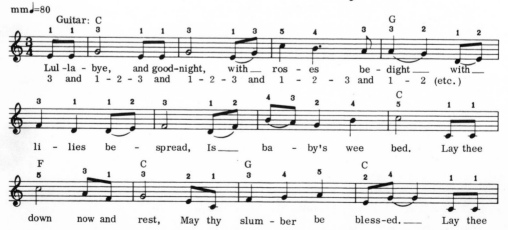

down now and rest, May thy slum - ber be blessed.
1 and uh 2 - 3 - 1 - 2.

I've Been Working on the Railroad

mm ♩=112

Guitar: C

I've ___ been work-ing on the rail - road, All ___ the live - long
Rhythm: 1 - 2 uh 3 uh 4 uh 1 - 2 - 3 - 4 (etc.)

day. I've ___ been work-ing on the rail - road, Just to pass the time a -

way; Can't ___ you hear the whis - tle blow - ing, Rise up so ear-ly in the

morn? Can't ___ you hear the cap-tain shout - ing ___ Di - nah blow your horn?

Dona Nobis Pacem (Grant Us Peace)

mm ♩=72

Guitar: C

Do - na no - bis pa - cem, pa - cem;

Do - na ___ no - bis pa - cem.

Pop Goes the Weasel

mm ♩.=126

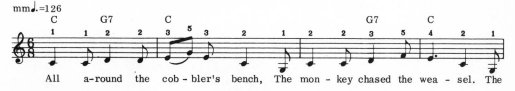

All a-round the cob - bler's bench, The mon - key chased the wea - sel. The

49

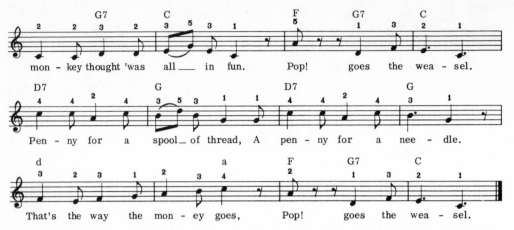

mon - key thought 'was all — in fun. Pop! goes the wea - sel.

Pen - ny for a spool — of thread, A pen - ny for a nee - dle.

That's the way the mon - ey goes, Pop! goes the wea - sel.

"Happy Fourth of July," the simple melody that follows, is actually tricky since it combines several meters: $\frac{2}{8}$ $\frac{3}{8}$ $\frac{3}{4}$ $\frac{7}{8}$ $\frac{2}{4}$. Many composers write in this style, and many old folk songs from Europe and the United States, composed unselfconsciously in an oral tradition, make use of this technique. It fits the natural accenting of the words. This one was made up spontaneously (as most folk songs are) by Michael Miller, age five:

Happy Fourth of July

mm ♩=152 The eighth note (♪) is constant throughout.

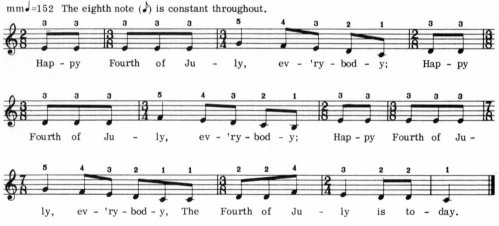

Hap - py Fourth of Ju — ly, ev - 'ry - bod - y; Hap - py

Fourth of Ju — ly, ev - 'ry - bod - y; Hap - py Fourth of Ju -

ly, ev - 'ry - bod - y, The Fourth of Ju — ly is to - day.

Hymn — Oh God Our Help in Ages Past

Oh God our help in a - ges past, Our hope for years to come,—

— Our re - fuge from the storm - y blast, And our e - ter - nal home.

Left hand to same hymn:

See if by now you wouldn't like to try both hands together on the same hymn again:

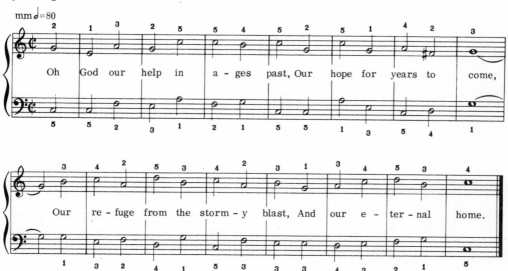

The last piece in this chapter was fun but represents another important level you've reached in teaching yourself to play: using both hands. In the next chapter you will develop this skill to add more interest and expressiveness to your playing.

S I X

Playing with Both Hands

Except for a few special examples, up to now we have been dealing with melody alone. The tune "Oh God Our Help in Ages Past" is a single line of music—and we have been using one finger at a time because we have been playing only one line of music.

In melody or linear music the notes literally follow each other singly, in one line. Linear music represents the simplest form of piano music.

Most music we listen to consists of two or more lines of notes played simultaneously. We hear *combined sounds* consisting of more than one note. This combining of notes gives music its richness and fullness.

So we must now begin to learn to play more complex music—music with two or more lines, and you must be able to play these lines simultaneously. This means you will often use two or more fingers of the same hand at the same time. More often than not, you will actually use two or more fingers *of both hands at once*—four or more fingers will be working.

How does music of more than two lines appear when written?

The following arrangement of the hymn you played in the preceding chapter—"Oh God Our Help in Ages Past"—shows you. To the two-part (one for each hand) version at the end of that chapter, let us add a third part. It is the bottom row of notes on the upper staff. Bottom row and top row are to be played simultaneously. The result is a fuller, richer sound. Try it. Practice until you can play it smoothly, using both hands:

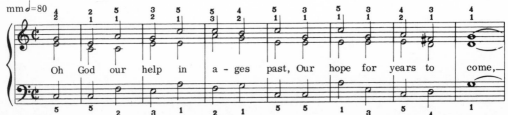

Once you can play that smoothly enough for your satisfaction (remembering that you are still your own critic), try the complete four-part version below. This version introduces two lines of music for each hand. Pay attention to the correct positioning of each finger before you strike the notes. Try to make all four notes sound simultaneously, striving for uniform volume and tone quality. This is a very essential element of good playing and good musicianship.

Note: When two or more notes are sounded simultaneously on the piano, the combination is called a *chord*.

HARMONY

Once again you have unobtrusively been doing something very important in mastering the piano.

You have been playing *harmony.*

By definition, when you play more than one note at a time, you are playing harmony. The chords you just played are an example.

Harmonization is the act of playing or singing or composing harmony to a melody. Since the time of Johann Sebastian Bach (1685-1750), harmonization in four parts has become a standard music practice. Bach's harmonizations of hymns (called chorales) are rich and expressive. They represent excellent study and practice examples for pianists and musicians at all levels (see Bibliography).

You might want to know something of how harmonization developed.

Some of the earliest music we know, the music of the ancient Greeks, for example, was *monophonic*. That is, it consisted of a single melody without accompaniment. Your own first attempts, striking one key at a time with one finger, was monophonic music.

A monophonic plain chant evolved in the Middle Ages out of the Greek scales, or modes. (The plain chant is still employed in Catholic services today, although polyphonic music—music of several lines played simultaneously—both instrumental and vocal, is performed as well.)

Gradually, over a period of about 300 years after the Middle Ages, church music was expanded vertically to include what we now call harmony (although secular music often made use of more than one voice or instrument). Growth was slow because the listener's ear adjusted only gradually to the new sounds.

Here is how the process evolved:

The first attempt to add another sound to the single line was the playing or singing of one long, held note during the performance of each section of the chant melody. A droning sound was produced. This drone technique is familiar today in Scottish bagpipe music, and you can duplicate it at the piano. (You can also do it singing with one other person.)

At the piano, try the line below. Sing C with an "ah" sound, as in father, while you play the main melody slowly. If you don't want to sing, play the note C with your left hand, and the melody with the right:

Play or sing: (Ah)

This C in the left hand, held as a drone, strongly emphasizes the tonality of the melody and has the greatest importance in the melody itself. It begins and ends single short phrases as well as the entire melody. It is the most natural single note to add in a melody played in the C major scale.

The next most natural and widely accepted note to add is the fifth note of the scale—the G in this case. (If you need to refresh your memory now, turn back to Chapter Two.) Interestingly, the fifth note of a scale is exactly the point where the vibrations of the string are divided in half—it is the second sound or note above the fundamental note in an overtone series. We call this note at an interval of a fifth from the tonic the dominant note.

The sound of two notes a fifth apart has always been felt to be a stable sound in many cultures. African tribesmen, joining in singing a melody that was too high or too low, have been reported to sing along at a fifth away—apparently without realizing that they were not singing the original melody.

54

In church singing the drone was produced by playing both the tonic (first) and the dominant (fifth) note along with the melody. Eventually the whole chant melody was harmonized at the interval of a fifth. This way of "organizing" composition into two simultaneously sounding parallel lines, a fifth apart, became known as two-part *organum.*

The use of the interval of the fifth to the exclusion of other intervals persisted for a very long time. Other intervals were felt to be harsh, dissonant, unstable. For two or three hundred years almost no piece of church music could begin or end with any other harmonization even when, later on, other intervals were permitted as passing notes from one important note to another.

From two-part organum there evolved a three-part form. Following is an example. Three-part organum sounds strange to our ears—empty, if not harsh. Yet in its time it was considered complex, up-to-date and rich. You might like to sing this with someone else or play it on the piano. The example is taken from "Schola Enchiriadis," a manuscript dated about A.D. 850.* The eyebrow mark above the long note is called a fermata. It tells the performer to hold the note for a long time, at his or the conductor's discretion, independently of the value of the note.

Toward the fourteenth century other notes were permitted in the harmony of beginning and ending chords in sacred music, although its gradual use in popular and secular music was already known.

That next note filled in the chord (made up, you will remember, of the tonic and the fifth notes) at the interval of a third from the tonic note. The sound of the three-note chord—called a *triad*—is familiar to everyone:

Interval of   Interval of
fifth: C-G   third: C-E

It consists of the tonic, C; the fifth, G; and, in the middle, filling out the harmony, the third note, E.

This chord sounds so solid and stable to our ears, I think, because it is made up of notes from the natural overtone series that are very closely related to the tonic. (In fact, the three notes of the chord C-E-G cover the six notes in the overtone series of C.)

G
E
C

C   C   G   C   E   Chord of C

* From Harvard Anthology of Music.

55

It *seems* very solid and stable to our ears. But it was a forbidden, almost sacrilegious sound in church music for a long, long time. Today it is one of the basic note formations of music and used often. Because of this wide usage it has become pleasant to hear, or as we say in musical terms, *consonant*.

But so are other, far more complex sounds, though they need the proper "surroundings." For example, play this sound:

If that sounds strange, add these notes to it . . .

. . . or play this:

Adding the extra note to the seemingly strange group of three notes fills out the harmony and "explains" the sound to our ears.

READY FOR MELODIES

The above demonstrates another characteristic of familiar music. It is only out of context that sounds or harmonies appear harsh. When they are properly "justified" to the ear as the notes played by the left hand above "explained" the notes played by the right hand, complex sounds can seem quite natural or "stable."

Having thought a little about the growth of harmony usage, we are now ready to try playing melodies with harmony at the piano.

One type of harmonization of a melody is the following: under a single melody played by the right hand is a group of two, three or four chords played by the left. These chords are changed to bring out the harmony, or richness, inherent in the melody.

The method for choosing the chords can be explained and taught to some degree, but the final choice is largely a matter of the player's intuition. The intuition, or "feeling," is completely mysterious to some, totally natural to others. It can be developed, sometimes easily, as countless beginning guitarists have found to be true. The easy development of an ability to harmonize accounts for much of the popularity the guitar has always enjoyed, long before it went electric and swept the country.

Here are some harmonizations of melodies you have already played.

Play all notes simultaneously, using both hands, and do not be discouraged by initial mistakes, for this is more difficult than anything you have played before.

Mary Had A Little Lamb

Twinkle, Twinkle, Little Star

For variety we can break up the accompanying chord and play a left hand which is especially suited to the guitar and often used on the piano:

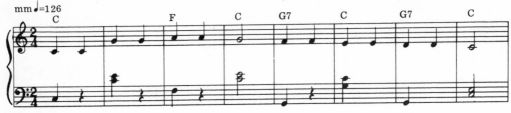

Some melodies seem to call for richer harmony in the accompaniment:

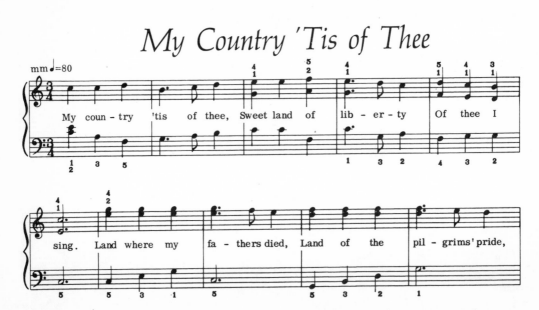

From ev - 'ry__ moun - tain side Let__ free - dom ring.

Here you began to play two notes at once in the right hand. Don't worry about getting everything perfect. Concentrate on matching the two hands.

Not all melodies are in the right hand:

Theme of *Schubert's Unfinished Symphony — First Movement (portion)*

Happy Farmer (portion)

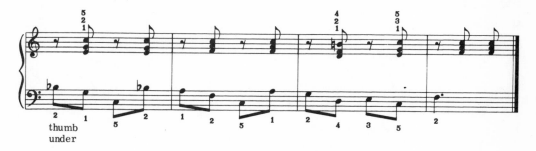

First, practice the left hand slowly, alone.

To develop your ability to move about freely with your left hand accompaniment, and also to show you how shifting accents and uneven phrases can make the music more interesting, here are two children's tunes in a slightly jazzy arrangement:

Eency Weency Spider

Een - cy ween-cy spi - der went up the wa - ter spout. Down came the
rain and it washed the spi-der out. Out came the sun and dried up all the
rain, And the een - cy ween-cy spi - der went up the spout a - gain.

Pop Goes the Weasel

All a-round the cob - bler's bench, the mon - key chased the wea - sel. The
mon - key thought 'twas all — in fun. Pop! goes the wea - sel.

60

For more independence of the hands, here is a round. Others can sing along or join in with instruments. First play line "a" alone; then add line "b" in the right hand; then add "c" playing all three lines at the same time.

The entire melody also can be sung by one person, singing first "a," then "b," then "c." For a round, the second voice begins "a" when the first reaches "b." The third enters when the first reaches "c."

Dona Nobis Pacem (Grant Us Peace)

W.A. MOZART

Here is a version of the Brahms "Lullaby" that uses broken chords (the notes of a chord played consecutively rather than simultaneously) in the left hand:

Brahms' Lullaby

DEVELOPMENT OF HARMONIC STYLE

The pieces you have been playing in this chapter have included sharps and flats—notes that were not in the original written music. The reason for this is that the development of harmonic style since the time of Bach has been a period of the gradual inclusion of more and more outside, or extra, notes into common musical practice. In the last 50 to 75 years this process has accelerated considerably.

Arnold Schönberg (1874-1951) started calling this music *12-tone* or *dodecaphonic* music at the end of World War One. He and others such as Anton Webern (1883-1945) and Alban Berg (1885-1935) wanted to justify the increased complexity of their music.

Regardless of written theories to support any music, and regardless of methods developed to justify one way of composing or another, it has always been the music which has come first, and the theory second. The ear was the original, and remains the ultimate, judge.

Musical history is a study in changing opinions and tastes. The musical style that probably seems most natural to you today was strange, perhaps even repugnant, to most listeners 150 years ago.

Beethoven's music was strange to most of his contemporaries. Now our ears accept it.

In the next chapter you will notice a gradual addition of sharps and flats to the music you will play; you will also find a new scale to go with each piece. Before moving ahead, however, you might like to hear a sample of sounds that are made up of complex intervals made possible by the use of sharps and flats. Try the following chords. Some of them have standard names and these are noted. As you learn more and more music in this book, and elsewhere, too, come back to try these chords again. They will probably seem more and more natural to you.

Chord built on 4th's   2 chords employing 6 notes
                                        each (12 different notes).

You are now at the stage when your practice will be more and more concerned with preparing whole pieces of music. You will study techniques, and new ideas and information, in the context of performing an entire musical work.

You should keep up your study of intervals. Practice the new scales that you will learn in the next and the following chapters.

But you have reached a point when you can start to build a small repertory, and your main efforts will be directed toward performing this music. This is an important turning point.

Congratulations!

---

* This symbol, ♮ called a natural sign, means that the note should be played as it is, neither sharp nor flat (for fuller explanation, see Chapter Seven).

SEVEN

Music in Some Major
Keys

You are ready to take some giant steps. In your practice of scales you will now be able to begin to learn a new scale every two or three days and to play music based on that scale. We will start with scales that contain sharps. Sharps and flats color music for us, and the term for music so enriched is "chromatic," from the Greek word *chroma,* meaning color.

ACCIDENTALS

In music, sharps (♯), flats (♭) and naturals (♮), along with double sharps (✗) and double flats (♭♭), are called "accidentals."

Before proceeding, here are definitions of the new terms in that last paragraph.

Natural—A natural is played neither sharp nor flat, but unchanged.

Double sharp, double flat—These are notations you may not see in much of the music you play. They appear rarely. But they do exist and you should at least know what they mean, even if it seems very complex at this stage. A double sharp ✗ means you must move the note two half-steps to the right. Thus F double sharp becomes G.

A double flat ♭♭ means move the note two half-steps to the left. Thus G double flat becomes F.

Now you are ready to move ahead into the major scales.

Major scales. There are easily a dozen different ways to build a scale. Each kind is called a *mode* and is named according to its sequence of half-steps and whole steps (see Chapter Three).

Certain modes were used during the time of the Greeks. Others were added or altered by the early Christian church. The church *modes*—Aeolian, Dorian, Phrygian, for example—may still be heard. Some composers of the twentieth century have written in ancient modes. The Beatles and other popular groups have done wonderful things with them. In a later chapter you will learn a song built from an ancient mode.

But the two modes that are the most often employed by composers since the early 1600s, which is the beginning of the musical period called the Baroque, are the *major* and the *minor*. Most of western music is built on major and minor scales. The major scale, as we have learned, is built on one particular sequence of half-steps and whole steps.

You will remember from Chapter Two that a major interval is larger than a minor interval. For example, a major third, comprising two whole steps, extends from C to E:

But a minor third, comprising a whole step and a half-step, extends from C to E-flat:

In a major scale (e.g., C major) the first three notes form the interval of a major third:

In a minor scale (e.g., C minor) the first three notes form a minor third:

The rest of this chapter will deal only with characteristics of the major scale and will introduce you to music built on several major scales. (In the next chapter we will look at some of the minor scales.)

In addition to the fact that the first three notes of a major scale form the interval of a major third, a major scale always has a half-step between the third and fourth notes and a half-step between the seventh and eighth notes. In the example above you'll see that this half-step occurs between the seventh note, B, and the C following it.

The seventh note of a major scale is called the *leading tone* because it leads back to the tonic note that gives the scale its name.

In order that the distance from the leading tone to the eighth note, or tonic, may *always* be a half-step, it may become necessary to raise the seventh white note and half-step toward the black note immediately to its right. So in the scale of G major, the seventh note—or leading tone, F—becomes F-sharp, and we say the scale of G major has one sharp:

KEY

When a piece of music is constructed principally of notes found in a given scale we say it is in the key with the same name as the scale. Such a piece, if it does not begin on the key note (the tonic), ends on it or at least on a note clearly harmonized with a chord that is based on it. A piece in G major usually ends on the note G. And the key of G major is also called the *tonality* of G major.

KEY SIGNATURE

We could write the sharps or flats in a piece of music in front of each note. But in music all the sharps or flats that are used regularly in the piece are written in a group—at the start of the piece and at the start of each staff throughout the piece. Writing these instructions just once at the beginning of the staff spares us a great deal of cluttered notation.

The sharps or flats appearing at the beginning of a staff are called the key signature:

When you see music so marked, play every F as F-sharp. Here is a little piece with one sharp in the signature. Always play F-sharp:

ARRANGED BY A. M.

(F-sharp in signature)

Key signature instructions are followed throughout the piece, obeyed for every note they cover.

There are certain specific exceptions, however. In the next diagram, the key signature tells us each F is to be played sharp, but notice the F in the middle measure. In front of it is the natural sign (♮).

Whenever an F natural is wanted in a piece that normally uses only F-sharp, the *natural* sign—♮—is put in front of that single note. The change or alteration of that note from sharp to natural then applies to every note F within that measure. In the next measure the original version of the note as indicated by the key signature is used. Here is the way this would be written:

F-sharp in time signature.

And here is how it would be played:

A single changed note, such as the F above, is known as a *special* accidental because there were no instructions covering the change in the key

66

signature. Special accidentals are also bound by rules. In the following music, notice the sprinkling of sharped A's throughout, even though the key signature calls only for F-sharps. All the A's are special accidentals:

Alexander's Ragtime Band

IRVING BERLIN

Come on a - long,＿＿come on a - long, Let me take you by the hand,

One rule for special accidentals is this: a special accidental sign before a note also affects every repeat of the note within that measure. Examine the segment from "Alexander's Ragtime Band" again. The first A in the first measure of the first staff is sharped. The second A is played sharp also. In this example, special accidental signs dominate the A's of the first three measures. The rule applies measure by measure.

When there are no special accidental instructions in a new measure, the orders of the original key signature are again in force.

Look at the fourth measure on the top staff. There is no special accidental sign and all A's in this measure are natural, since nothing in the original signature tells us to play A any other way. (Note: The bottom staff in this example merely repeats the top, with playing instructions again spelled out in detail and with extra symbols that do not normally appear in written music.)

Now that you have seen how sharps are notated, let us turn to scales using sharps, and pieces built on these scales. Then we'll try some flats.

LEARNING SCALES WITH SHARPS

Following are examples of a few more scales with sharps. From now on, exercises and ideas will be introduced at a faster rate, and more and more actual music will be included in your learning. Each scale will be accompanied by music using its notes in the composition. Each piece of music introduces a difficulty you have not yet encountered.

However, your learning pace should continue to be steady and gradual. Play each scale for ten minutes or so at a time. Do not move on to the next scale until you have mastered both the scale *and* the accompanying music.

Your head will now urge you forward faster than your fingers can take you. Resist. Try to be thorough and disciplined. Don't skip. How long a time you actually spend depends upon your ability, but two or three days on a scale and its accompanying music will be the minimum time. Try to do something at the piano each day. If you miss one day's practice, go back to the previous scale and its music. Practice them until you are certain of them again and work forward from there.

G Major: We saw above that G major has one sharp—F-sharp.

D Major: here is the scale of D major with its two sharps—F-sharp and C-sharp—notated in the key signature.

Earlier, you played part of a theme from the first movement of Schubert's Unfinished Symphony. Here is the entire melody (played by the left hand) in its original key of D major. Be careful of the added D-sharps in the left hand and the B-flat in the right hand.

Measures one and two are notated differently from the following measures, to help explain their off-the-beat, or *syncopated*, quality. In all of the following pieces, the fingerings, where they depart from normal scale fingerings, help you to insure the position of the hand.

Symphony No. 9 (Unfinished)

FRANZ SCHUBERT

A Major: the scale of A major has three sharps—F-sharp, C-sharp and G-sharp.

Right hand.

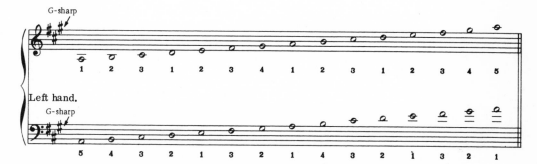

Now try this opening section of the Mozart A-major sonata. The rhythm is usually the same in both hands, but there are sometimes more than one note for one hand, with a different rhythm required.

Sonata in A Major

W. A. MOZART

sf - sforzando (a sudden slight accent)

p - piano (softly)

SCALES WITH FLATS

By now it should be a week or two since you started on sharps with the D major scale and Schubert's Unfinished Symphony. You are ready for major scales written with flats. Follow the same practicing advice given you when you took up sharps: don't skip; be disciplined; practice each scale in ten-minute sessions for at least three days. And learn the scale and the accompanying music well before you move ahead.

The scales that have only a few flats may seem easy to you after scales with all those sharps, but the music accompanying them continues to escalate in difficulty and to present you with new playing problems.

F Major: F major has one flat—B-flat:

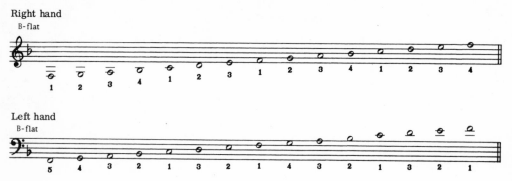

Here it is in "Silent Night." Notice the different groupings in the right hand. Keep the music smooth.

Silent Night

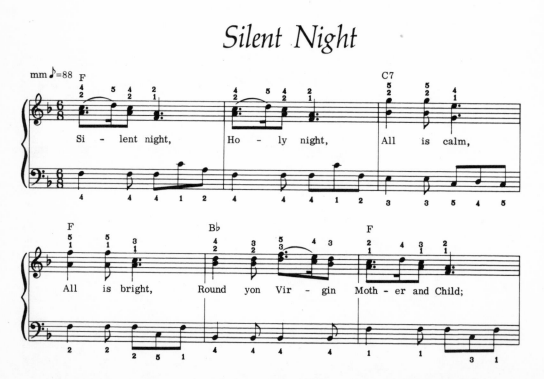

70

Ho — ly In — fant so tender and mild Sleep in heav — en — ly

peace,_____ Sleep__ in heav — en — ly peace._____

B♭ Major: B♭ major has two flats—B-flat and E-flat:

Play it in "The Soldier's March" from *Faust,* by Charles Gounod (below). Note that big skip in the left hand and when you play, make sure the music retains its gusto.

The Soldier's March *(from* FAUST)

CHARLES GOUNOD

mm♩.=100

E♭ Major: E♭ major has three flats—B-flat, E-flat and A-flat:

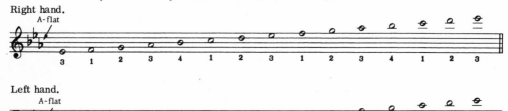

The hymn below has four individual lines which together make a very rich harmonization. Try to hear each line as you play. The middle line of the left hand may occasionally be played in the right.

Harmonization of
All Glory, Laud and Honor

J. S. BACH

This sign means repeat from beginning.

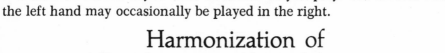

A♭ Major: A♭ major has four flats—B-flat, E-flat, A-flat and D-flat:

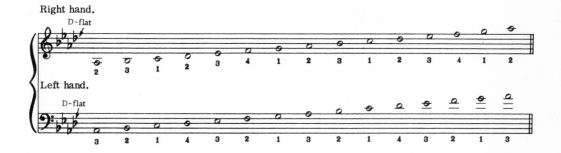

Now try it in:

My Wild Irish Rose

Words and Music by HAUNCEY OLCOTT

mm ♩=132

My wild I - rish Rose,———— The sweet-est flow'r that

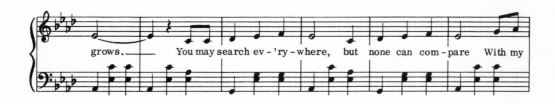

grows.———— You may search ev-'ry-where, but none can com-pare With my

wild I - rish Rose.———— My wild I - rish Rose,————

73

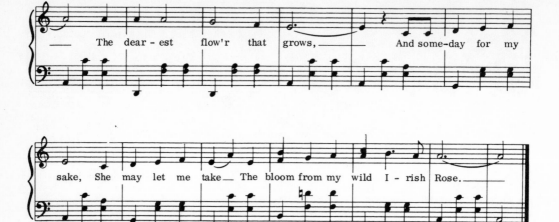

The rest of the major keys are more complicated and will be dealt with in Chapter Nine. First we will take up some scales and music in the easier minor keys.

EIGHT

Minor Scales and Keys

There are two kinds of minor scales. Both are widely used in musical composition. One is the *harmonic minor* and the other is the *melodic minor*. Both have their origins in the early church modes and have been common in music from the time of J. S. Bach (1685-1750) to the present.

HARMONIC MINOR

The harmonic minor was created by adding a leading tone to what we call the old Aeolian mode which, as you will recall, is the scale of white notes beginning and ending on A:

As evident in the above scale, when the seventh note, G, is sharped, placing it a half-step from A, it becomes a leading tone. The change creates the harmonic minor scale. Note that there is an interval of a minor third between the first note, A, and the third note, C. Notice also that there is a half-step between the fifth note, E, and the sixth note, F:

MELODIC MINOR

During the early years of music in the Christian church, musicians felt that the interval of a minor third from F to G-sharp was awkward to sing. So they changed the scale a little. They kept the G-sharp, but in going from E upward they made F into F-sharp. Now there was no longer a skip of a minor third from the fifth note to the sixth note:

But in descending passages, the F natural was left alone; and the G-sharp, since it no longer had to lead upward to A, was changed back to G natural. The descending version of this melodic minor scale is therefore the same as the original Aeolian mode, as follows:

In this way, the melodic minor scale developed two forms—one for ascending passages and another for descending ones. To the player, this means there are also two sets of fingerings, one for ascending and one for descending.

The melodic minor creates a smoother transition from F to G-sharp. The harmonic minor is used in a melody where the skip from F to G-sharp does not have to be made or where the harmony under the melodic line can help to smooth it out.

Here is a piece especially written to give you an idea how the two forms of the minor can be used:

Piece in A Minor

A. M.

Observe where G♯ is used and where the G is natural. In this slide technique play the note B with the 4th finger and slide to the fifth without releasing the note. This shifts the hand and makes all four remaining fingers available. In the above music, also see if you can find segments of the harmonic minor scale and the two forms of melodic minor. If you need help, refer to the three preceding examples in this chapter.

KEY SIGNATURE FOR MINOR SCALES

You already know that the key signature is the group of sharps or flats that appear at the beginning of a piece. (Sometimes no sharps or flats are indicated, as in C major.) *The signature of a piece in a minor key is taken from the descending version of the melodic minor scale.*

Music in A minor has no sharps or flats in the signature—descending A melodic minor scale:

A piece in E minor has one sharp (F-sharp)—descending E melodic minor scale:

A piece in D minor has one flat (B-flat)—descending D melodic minor scale:

By custom, the key signature is always written in a uniform way, even if certain individual notes are sharped or flatted every time they appear in a given piece of music.

MINOR KEYS WITH SHARPS

Further below is some familiar music in E minor. It is the Christmas carol called "God Rest You Merry, Gentlemen." It shows nicely how certain notes change, even though not ordered so in the key signature. F-sharp is in the signature. D-sharp is the leading tone and occurs often in the melody, although D natural is used several times to harmonize other chords.

But before trying it, learn and practice the E minor scales following:

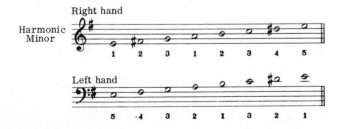

God Rest You Merry, Gentlemen

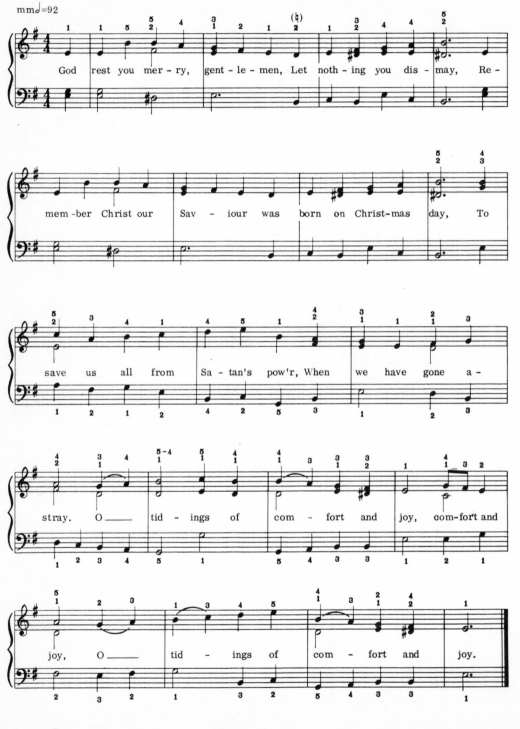

RELATIVE MINOR

Certain major and minor keys have the same key signature and these are said to be related to each other. For example, the major key related to A minor is C major; neither has any sharps or flats in the key signature.

The scale of a minor therefore is called the relative minor of C major; and C major is called the relative major of A minor.

The relative minor of G major (one sharp) is E minor.

The relative major of D minor (one flat) is F major.

You will find the complete table of relative majors and minors in the Appendix.

Now you will learn more minor scales and pieces in several minor keys. First we do the minor keys with sharps, and then the minor keys with flats.

B Minor: B minor has two sharps—F and C. Its relative major is D major. The leading tone is A ♯.

Right hand
Melodic minor

Harmonic minor

Left hand
Melodic minor

Harmonic minor

Here is a short piece in B minor with a slightly tricky left. Try to keep the crossing smooth.

A. M.

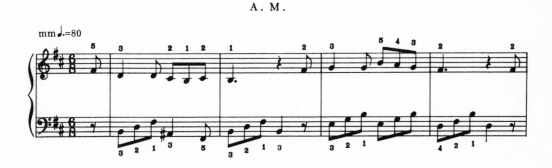

F-Sharp Minor: F-sharp minor has three sharps—F, C and G. Its relative major is A major and its leading tone is E♯.

Right hand
Melodic minor

Harmonic minor

Left hand
Melodic minor

Harmonic minor

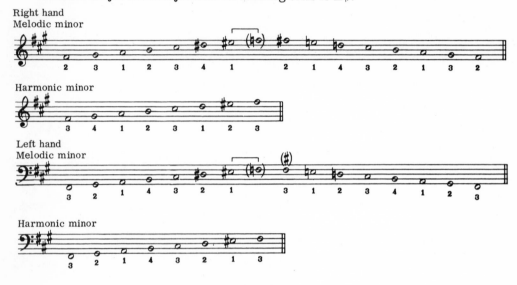

Try it in:

Song of the Volga Boatmen

ARRANGED BY A. M.

Andante (moving easily) mm ♩=84

This line is a slur. It means sing all on one syllable. Yo,— heave ho. Yo,— heave ho. All to - geth - er— now.

Yo,— heave ho. See the bir - ches on yon - der shore.

Pull my sail-ors— more and more. Ai la-la, ai - la, Pull all to-geth - er—

Tie this note over.

quarter rest

This is a fermata.
It means *hold*.

_Pull to - geth - er— now, Yo — heave ho. —

For variation, try playing the final A in the left hand as A-sharp and see how you like it. Sometimes pieces in minor keys end in major to give a solid effect.

Did you notice, starting with the ninth measure of this song, that the left hand plays the melody two beats later than the right hand? This "imitation" of one hand, or "voice," by another, when it is exact imitation, is called a canon, or a round. A canon or round is a composition in two or more voice parts, employing imitation in its strictest form.

MINOR KEYS WITH FLATS

D Minor: D minor has one flat—B♭. Its relative major is F major; its leading tone is C♯.

D minor
Right hand

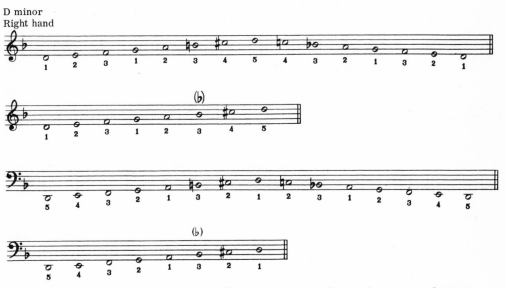

From now on certain pieces will leave much of the fingering choices to you.

Minuet

J. S. BACH

(from Anna Magdalena Song Book—see Bibliography)

Bach's original composition contains an extra measure at the end of each half (before the double bar in the middle, and before the end) that leads back to repeating the same half.

Note the use of elements of the melodic and harmonic minors, depending upon the direction (up or down) of the scale.

Notice also that the first half of this minuet—up to the double bar after measure 8—moves from D minor to F major—its relative major. The second half returns to D minor. This moving from key to key is called modulation and makes for interest and variety.

G Minor: G minor has two flats—B and E. Its relative major is B major; its leading tone is F♯.

You learned to sing "Go Down, Moses" in school. Now play it in G minor:

Go Down, Moses

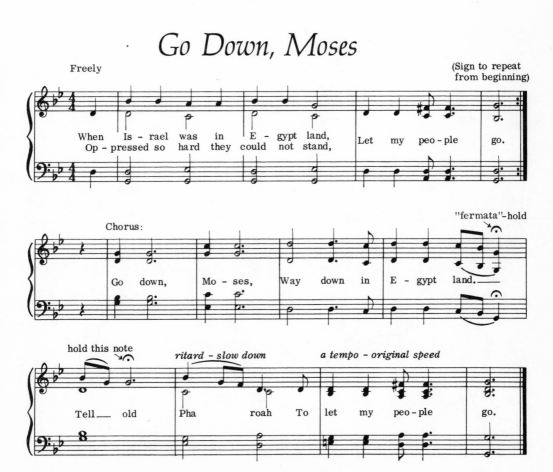

C Minor: C minor has three flats—B-flat, E-flat, A-flat. Its relative major is E♭; its leading tone is B natural.

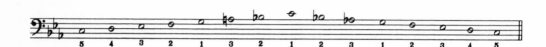

Try it now in this Chopin Prelude in C Minor. This will give you practice in reading ledger lines at the bottom of the left-hand staff, and I hope it will be made easier because the left hand is all in octaves. Try practicing the left hand alone first.

Prelude in C Minor

FREDERIC CHOPIN
Opus. 28, No. 20

There are several things to consider when playing the above music:
(1) The *crescendo* in the second bar means "play louder." (2) The arrow-shaped mark appearing between the two staves of the last measure signifies *diminuendo*, or softer. Let this note die out while holding down the right pedal. (3) Try to keep the octaves smooth (*legato*) in the left hand.

At the same time, play the right-hand chords firmly.

In the next chapter we will go back and finish all the rest of the major and minor keys.

NINE

The Remaining Major and Minor Keys

Here is the scale of B major. It has 5 sharps: F-sharp, C-sharp, G-sharp, D-sharp and A-sharp.

Right Hand

Left hand

And here it is used in "On Top of Old Smoky" (note the crossing left hand with skips):

On Top of Old Smoky

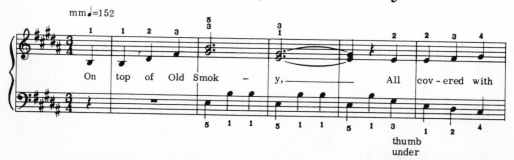

The key of F♯ major has 6 sharps: F-sharp, C-sharp, G-sharp, D-sharp, A-sharp and E-sharp.

Try it in "Dixie," put here to develop agility in a tough key. Don't let the skips in the left hand slow you down.

Dixie

The key of C ♯ major has 7 sharps: F-sharp, C-sharp, G-sharp, D-sharp, A-sharp, E-sharp and B-sharp.

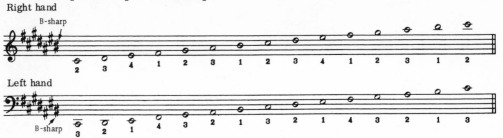

Try "I've Been Working on the Railroad." This is an easy melody but has a hard left hand—until you figure out the right notes.

I've Been Working on the Railroad

Now back to major keys with flats. You will remember that in Chapter Seven we aready met F, B-flat, E-flat and A-flat major.

The key of D♭ major has 5 flats: B-flat, E-flat, A-flat, D-flat, and G-flat.

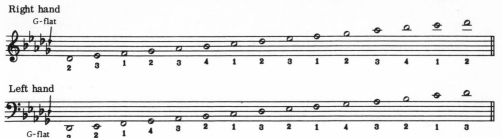

Here is the "Thanksgiving Hymn," in D-flat major. Practice the left hand alone. Play it as smoothly as possible. The right hand requires sliding from one finger to another on one note, while holding another note. We introduced the technique in Chapter Eight, but it is very important here. This smooth, sustained *legato* playing keeps the voices independent and the melodies sustained. A certain amount of stretching and sliding will be necessary. Be sure to hold the longer notes while others change.

Thanksgiving Hymn

The key of G♭ has 6 flats: B-flat, E-flat, A-flat, D-flat, G-flat and C-flat.

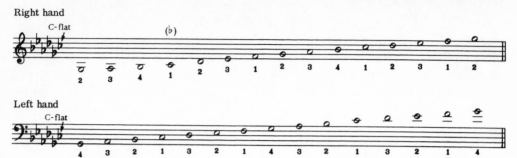

Here is "Gaudeamus Igitur," an old student song. The double bar with two dots :‖ means go back and repeat the section in front of it. This arrangement uses full chords and octaves. Learn to play it vigorously, yet with dignity, not harshly.

Gaudeamus Igitur

The scale of C-sharp minor has four sharps: F-sharp, C-sharp, G-sharp and D-sharp. Its leading tone is B-sharp (C natural). Its relative major is E major.

Here is "Greensleeves," a haunting piece you probably already know. Maintain a smooth line with the left hand. This piece will give you practice in reading lower ledger lines played by the right hand.

"Greensleeves" also contains a good example of the use of the melodic minor (in measure seven, where A-sharp is employed). Did you notice how the ninth measure is written in the relative E major key? Also, the sharps and naturals in parentheses are sometimes played, sometimes sung. Try them. They give a different flavor.

This English folk song is at least four hundred years old, and there is a reference to it in Shakespeare's *The Merry Wives of Windsor*. Falstaff says at one point:

> Let the skies rain potatoes,
> Let it thunder to the tune of "Greensleeves."

Be careful of the fingering, especially of the crossings in measures seven, nine, 13 and 15.

Greensleeves

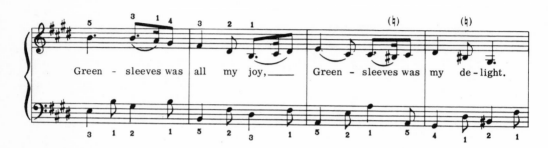

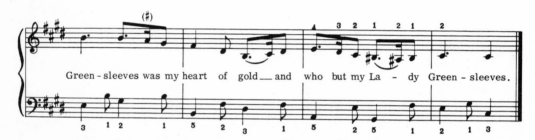

The scale of G-sharp minor has five sharps: F-sharp, C-sharp, G-sharp, D-sharp and A-sharp. Its leading tone is F-double-sharp (written F✗ or G♮). Its relative major is B major.

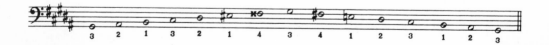

Notice that you have encountered your first regular use of a double sharp. This is notated as above (F✗). On the piano, F-double-sharp is played as G natural. If the note were written G natural (G♮) it could be confused with G-sharp (G♯).

I have written a simple piece for you to provide an easy introduction to the use of F-double-sharp. This piece is also an exercise in observing ties, so keep everything *legato*—smooth.

Soliloquy
A. M.

CHANGING PATTERNS, HARMONIC COLORS

Now we return to the minor keys with flats. In Chapter Eight we stopped with C minor, which has three flats. To go on:

The scale of F minor has four flats: B, E, A and D. Its leading tone is E natural. The relative major of F minor is A-flat major.

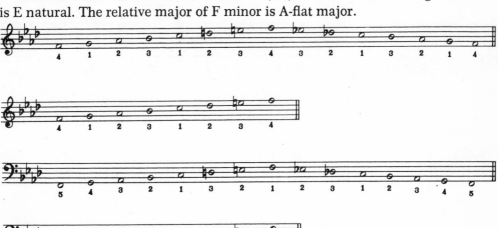

93

This next piece—a canon, or round—not only uses the F minor scale but also will help you to develop better independence of each hand from the other. Each line is actually the same music, but the right hand begins playing two beats later than the left.

You were introduced to such music in the accompaniment to the "Song of the Volga Boatmen," in which part of the left-hand line imitated the right. This round can go on forever, one line exactly the same as the other. In fact, it is a canon in perpetual motion. If you repeat what is written from first double bar to second double bar, it never ends. When you want to end it, simply play the second ending.

Canon in Perpetual Motion

A. M.

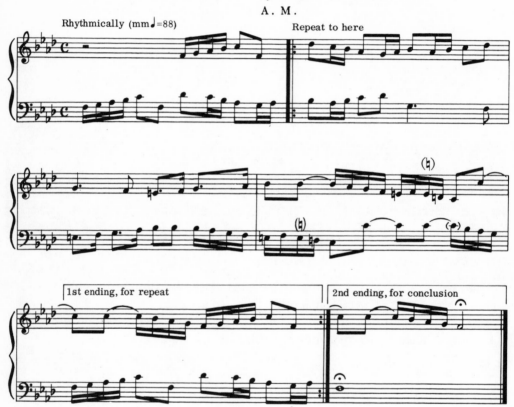

Now we come to the scale of B flat minor. It has five flats—B-flat, E-flat, A-flat, D-flat and G-flat. Its leading tone is A natural. The relative major is D-flat major.

94

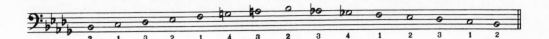

The folk song that follows, "The Wayfaring Stranger," looks deceptively easy. It was chosen to help develop greater independence of your hands.

The melody of the first part is played by the left hand. Be alert for the small changes in the right hand. In the second part, beginning with bar eight, the melody shifts to the right hand.

Be careful. You may find the left hand very tricky. Any measure by itself is easy, but the small changes in the pattern from measure to measure may fool you.

There are many versions of this melody. This particular one shows you the possibilities for harmonic color. Notice that the leading tone is never used in the melody. Like many folk songs in this country and in England, the melody is neither major nor minor, but modal from some early mode—in this case, the Aeolian mode.

Play this as freely as you can. Go faster in places as your mood dictates; slow down in others. This style is termed *rubato*, from the Italian *rubare*—to rob. You are in effect robbing time in one part of the music by playing fast, paying it back in another by playing slowly.

The Wayfaring Stranger

ARRANGED BY A. M.

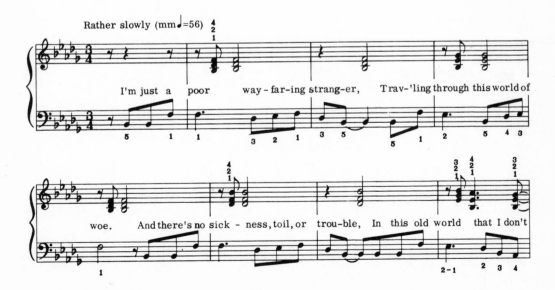

know. I'm go-ing back   to see my moth-er.   I'm go-ing there,   no more to

espressivo ("with expression" - slow down, or dwell on these notes to help the harmony sound through.)

roam. I'm just a - go - ing o-ver Jor-dan. I'm just a - go - ing o-ver home.

Finally we come to the scale of E-flat minor, which can also be called D-sharp minor. Somehow, as E-flat minor, it seems easier to deal with.

E-flat minor has six flats—B-flat, E-flat, A-flat, D-flat, G-flat and C-flat (B natural). The leading tone is D natural. The relative major is G-flat major. (If you choose to call this scale D-sharp minor, its relative major is F-sharp major.)

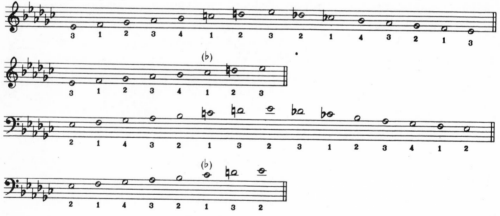

For practice in the E-flat minor scale, this "Solemn March" is useful:

Solemn March

A. M.

Did you notice that in the eighth bar the piece modulated, or shifted, from E-flat minor to its relative major, G-flat major? This provides contrast of tone color and atmosphere.

You have now encountered every major and minor key on the piano and you have also learned many pieces of music. You probably know more about how music is put together than those who study the piano by rote and "osmosis" for years as children.

In the remaining chapter you will learn nine more pieces and you will learn a large number of musical terms you have not needed until now. Also waiting for you are intricacies of tempo (speeding up and slowing down) and new markings that call for special interpretive effects.

When you have come this far you can easily handle the material ahead. Have a good time!

TEN

More and More Music

You've come far! Here are more pieces for you to enjoy. They are presented in the order in which they were composed, and not necessarily in the order of difficulty. Together they offer you a cross section of styles. Some may be tricky to play at first, but each can be mastered fairly quickly if you are patient and careful. (To find out more about each composer's life and times, and more about music by him, check the Bibliography in the back.)

Johann Sebastian Bach
(1685-1750)

From 1717 to 1723 Johann Sebastian Bach was organist, choirmaster and composer-in-residence at Köthen, Germany. In 1722 he wrote 24 preludes and fugues in each of the 12 major and minor keys and assembled them in a collection called *The Well-Tempered Clavier*. He intended them to be study pieces, each to develop compositional techniques as well as performing skills.

"Tempering" was the term for tuning the clavier, or clavichord, or any keyboard instrument. *The Well-Tempered Clavier* was Bach's reference to a new method of tuning introduced at that time, which made it feasible to play a keyboard instrument—the harpsichord, mainly—in all keys. Previously a harpsichord tuned in one key—C major, for example—did not sound well played in another—say, A major. The note E, when accurately tuned an interval of a major third from C, might not sound as well when tuned an interval of a fifth from A.

98

For Bach, a prelude is a short introductory piece. It is often the introduction to some larger work, as the word indicates, but it can and does often stand alone. A fugue is a piece with several melodic lines, or voices. The main melody—called a subject—is handed from one line to another according to certain general practices.

In 1744 Bach was in Leipzig and compiled a second volume of *The Well-Tempered Clavier* with 24 more preludes and fugues.

The following prelude, the first in Volume I, is well known. It contains no dynamic or tempo markings. Bach seldom wrote them, leaving these questions to the musical judgment of the performer. Do not use the right, sustaining pedal and keep the tone even. Hold the notes in the left hand as indicated.

Prelude

J. S. BACH

Wolfgang Amadeus Mozart

(1756-1791)

Wolfgang Amadeus Mozart was a child prodigy who began composing and playing the piano when he was five or six years old.

The following two short minuets for piano were among the first pieces he composed. A minuet is a graceful piece in $\frac{3}{4}$ time.

The Minuet in G Major was composed in 1761 or 1762, when Mozart was six or younger, and introduces you to two new terms. Note, at the end of the fourth line, the word *fine;* it means "end" in Italian. At the end of the piece there appears the phrase *da capo,* meaning "from the beginning." When you see *da capo,* go back to the beginning of the piece and play it again, without the repeats to the finish word, *fine.*

In 1862, after lengthy study, Ludwig von Köchel catalogued all Mozart's works in the chronological order in which they were written. This catalogue is known as the "Köchel Listing." According to him, this minuet is the first piece Mozart wrote. The catalogue, incidentally, was revised by Albert Einstein in 1937. Today Mozart's compositions are always identified by their numbers on the Köchel catalogue as well as by their names. This piece is therefore listed as "K. 1."

Minuet in G Major

W. A. MOZART (K.1)

da Capo
(go back to beginning
and play without re-
peats to Fine.)

Minuet in F Major was composed in January 1762. Its first half is eight measures long, repeated. The second half is the same length, but is notated in full and does not repeat. Notice how the entire piece is composed in four-measure segments, or phrases.

Minuet in F Major

W. A. MOZART (K.2)

Ludwig van Beethoven

(1770-1827)

Beethoven's style of writing for the piano, even in this very simple piece, is immediately recognizable as different from Mozart's or Bach's. Somehow the sound of his music is as much his own as his signature. In this famous beginner's work, the dynamics are important. I have included only the opening section.

Be alert for the triplets before the return to Tempo I toward the end. Instead of dividing the eighth note into two sixteenth notes, Beethoven divides it into *three* sixteenth notes. The eighth note continues to have the same time value, even though divided into three. The triplet is played in the same time it usually takes to play two sixteenths.

Für Elise (portion)
(for Elise)

LUDWIG VAN BEETHOVEN

a tempo (original tempo)

Robert Schumann

(1810-1856)

Robert Schumann wrote a great deal of piano music in addition to four symphonies, several concertos and many songs. One of the most famous piano compositions for beginners is his sprightly piece "Happy Farmer Returning From Work." Be sure to keep the accompaniment softer than the melody.

Happy Farmer Returning From Work

ROBERT SCHUMANN

Frisch und munter
Allegro animato – spirited

Roll the notes from the bottom

Frederic Chopin

(1810-1849)

Chopin wrote 24 preludes for the piano, none intended to precede larger pieces. All are short "mood" pieces of very free form. The following one is deceptively simple.

The very slow-moving notes in the right hand must be played as a sustained, singing melody. The subtly shifting harmonies of the left hand must be articulated so as to lend color and support to the right hand without being obtrusive. A slight *rubato* (speeding up and slowing down) is desirable.

You will also meet two new signs. In measure 16 you meet the ∾ This is called a turn and indicates a certain decoration of the note preceding it, as shown in this example.

The double sharp under the ∾ symbol instructs you *not* to play G-sharp:

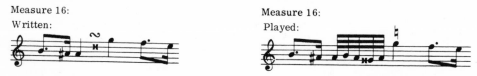

The second sign, in measure 17, is the word "Ped." This refers to the sustaining, or right, foot pedal. The asterisk (*) means you must release the pedal at the point where it appears, so as not to blur the harmony.

Notice also the triplet in measure 18.

Prelude

FREDERIC CHOPIN

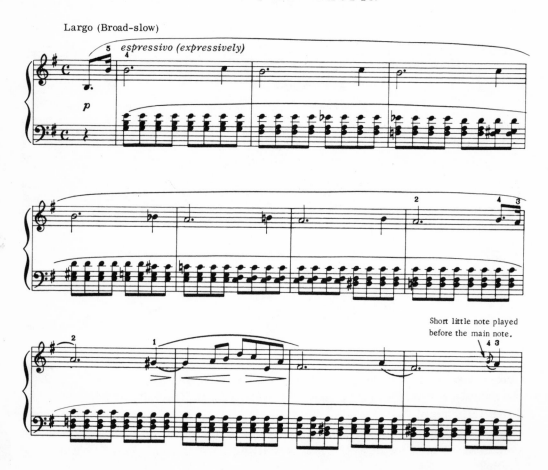

Johannes Brahms

(1833-1897)

Brahms' piano works are among his most expressive music. This waltz is
the second from a group of early pieces, Opus 39. When you are playing it,
strive for three different sound qualities: with the right hand, try to produce singing octaves. With the left hand, sustain the long notes through
each measure. Also with the left hand, play the shorter notes lightly, to
achieve a graceful, lilting rhythm under the singing right-hand octaves.

Waltz

JOHANNES BRAHMS
(Op. 39, No. 2)

Bela Bartok
(1881-1945)

One of the most important composers of the twentieth century, Béla Bartók was also a fine pianist and music educator. With his Hungarian countryman, Zoltan Kodály (1882-1967), Bartók published and recorded an enormous amount of folk music, and he drew upon folk themes in his own compositions.

This piece is from a collection of easy works for beginning pianists, based on Hungarian folk songs. It consists of a theme (*tema*) and three variations. Each variation presents the original theme in a different setting. The last variation changes meter from $\frac{3}{4}$ to $\frac{2}{4}$, so be alert for it.

If you find this sample of Bartók pleasant, you might also enjoy his six volumes of graded pieces for beginning and more advanced pianists, called *Mikrokosmos*.

Variations
BELA BARTOK

Norman Cazden
(1941-)

Here is some fun with changing meter. A hint: the eighth note retains
the same value throughout. The composer, Norman Cazden, was born in
the United States and has written music for all kinds of instrumental
combinations, large and small. Among his teachers were Walter Piston and
Aaron Copland.

Game

NORMAN CAZDEN

Milton Babbitt

(1916-)

Milton Babbitt is the foremost American exponent of a certain style of carefully planned compositional technique. In this style the music is written according to numerical patterns that are organized before composing the music. Babbitt has also composed a great deal of "electronic" music, using the RCA Synthesizer, a sound-producing machine operated jointly by Columbia and Princeton Universities. He is Professor of Music at Princeton.

This Duet for left and right hand (a twelve-tone work) will introduce you to a style of chromatic writing you have not met before in this volume.

Duet
For Betty Ann
MILTON BABBITT

116

APPENDIX

Major and minor scales with the same sharps and flats are said to be related to each other—or relative. The major key related to A minor is C major, for example; neither has any sharps or flats. The relative minor of G major is E minor; both have one sharp. The relative major of D minor is F major; both have one flat. Below is the complete chart of relative major and minor keys.

Chart of Relative Major and Minor Keys

No. of Sharps (read down)		MAJOR	MINOR
0		C	A
1		G	E
2		D	B
3		A	F♯
4		E	C♯
5		B	G♯
6	6	F♯ - G♭	D♯ - E♭
7	5	C♯ - D♭	B♭
	4	A♭	F
	3	E♭	C
	2	B♭	G
	1	F	D
	0	C	A
No. of Flats (read up)		MAJOR	MINOR

KEY: Sharp - ♯   Flat - ♭

GLOSSARY

Accidental—sharp (♯), flat (♭), double sharp (✗), double flat (♭♭) or natural (♮) note.

Bar line—the vertical line on a staff that separates one measure from the next.

Bass—the low instruments or voices. The bass clef (𝄢) appears on the five-line staff used by low instruments, as well as on music for the left hand of the piano.

Beat—the pulse felt in all music. It need not always be steady or regular, although it is so in most western music.

Binary—two-part.

Chord—two or more notes sounding simultaneously.

Chromatic—referring to notes in a piece that are not in the key signature. The chromatic scale proceeds by half-steps.

Clef—symbol placed at the beginning of the five-line staff, indicating the pitches to be represented by that particular staff. The piano staves, with their appropriate clefs, are:

Color—the quality of a sound by which we recognize and distinguish the instrument, or the combinations of instruments or voices, that produce the sound.

Compound time—a division of a measure that mixes combinations of two's and three's. For example: 6/8 divides a measure basically in half 6/8 | ♩. ♩. |

Each of these halves is made of three eighth notes: 6/8 | ♫♪ ♫♪ |

Consonant—opposite of dissonant, a highly subjective judgment, based on experience and taste, of the pleasant or conventionally harmonious quality of any sound.

Crescendo—getting louder.

Decrescendo—getting softer; synonymous with diminuendo.

Diminuendo—getting softer; synonymous with decrescendo.

Dissonant—a subjective description of (conventionally) unharmonious sounds.

Dodecaphonic—twelve-tone (see twelve-tone).

Dominant—the fifth note of a scale; also the chord based on the fifth note.

Dot—a small point the size of a period, placed to the right of a note, which increases the time value of the note by half: ♩. = ♩+♪   ♪. = ♪+♪

Downbeat—the strongest pulse at the beginning of a measure; it can be preceded by an upbeat (see upbeat).

Drone—a long-held note, over which other music proceeds, as in a bagpipe.

118

Dynamics—referring to loud and soft.

Ensemble—a group of instruments or performers; also indicates whether a group is playing well together.

Fermata—the symbol ⌒ over a note, instructing the performer to hold the note beyond its indicated time value (from the Italian *fermare*).

Flat—a symbol (♭) indicating the lowering of a note by a half-step; on the piano this means one key to the left. Flat also refers to inaccurate pitch that is mistakenly lower than it should be.

Grace note—a short ornamental note with no specified duration, played as fast as possible to decorate the note that follows it: ♪♩

Half note—♩ (see whole note).

Half-step—the distance between any note and the note immediately adjacent to it. On the piano the distance—up or down—from any note to its immediate neighbor, black or white, is a half-step.

Harmony—two or more notes sounding together, or combining to form a chord; the "vertical" aspect of music, if melody is the "horizontal" aspect.

Homophonic—literally, "the same sound"; refers to music of more than one voice but sounded at the same time. Chords played one after the other produce music which is homophonic.

Interval—the distance between any two notes.

Key—a harmonic center of a piece, based on a chord that bears the name of the key. The name of the key also applies to the first note, or tonic, of a scale, which helps to define the key.

Key signature—the sharps or flats appearing at the beginning of a piece of music, and at the beginning of each line of the piece, designating the sharps or flats to be played consistently throughout the piece.

Leading tone—the seventh note of a scale, one-half step below the return to the tonic, hence leading to the tonic.

Ledger lines—short lines parallel to the five-line staff to permit notation of pitches that are too high or too low for the staff.

Legato—Italian for "tied" or "connected"; indicates smooth, connected playing; the opposite of staccato (see staccato).

Major—denoting (1) intervals larger than minor, and (2) scales and keys in which the first three notes of the scale form a major third.

Major scale—a succession of steps proceeding upward as follows: whole step, whole step, half-step, whole step, whole step, whole step, half-step.

Measure—a unit of musical time containing the pattern of the strongest beat followed by weaker beats, and separated from the beginning of the next measure by a vertical bar line.

Melody—a succession of notes, or tones, or pitches.

Meter—the regular time pattern of strong and weak notes within a measure, for example: $\frac{2}{4}$ $\frac{3}{4}$ $\frac{6}{8}$ $\frac{9}{4}$

Metronome marking—the indication at the beginning of a piece telling where to set the beat of the metronome, an instrument that guides you in regulating the proper tempo. The metronome currently in use was invented by Mälzel in 1816. Beethoven was the first composer to make use of one.

Minor—denoting (1) intervals smaller than major, and (2) scales and keys in which the first three notes form a minor third.

Minor scale—a succession of notes, the first three forming a minor third, and the remaining organized according to a certain order of half-steps and whole steps. There are melodic minor scales and harmonic minor scales (see text for fuller explanation).

Mode—the particular oganization of scales according to the placement of half-steps and whole steps. The major mode and the minor mode are the two most commonly used today in western music. Medieval church music made use of others, including the Aeolian, Dorian, Phrygian, Lydian and Mixolydian.

Monophonic—literally, one sound; refers to a single line of music, or single voice (see polyphonic).

Motive—a short melodic fragment that establishes a recognizable pattern, either melodic or rhythmic or both. The famous

of Beethoven's Fifth Symphony is a motive.

Octava—a symbol (8va⌐----) indicating that the performance of notes under the dotted line should be one octave higher than notated. When written 8va _____ the notes should be played one octave lower.

Octave—the distance spanned by eight notes, that is, from any note to the recurrence in a scale of the note with the same name.

Organum—medieval church music from the ninth to the middle of the thirteenth century, in which one or more composed parts were added to a plain-chant melody.

Overtones—pitches present in any sounded note, produced by the medium vibrating simultaneously in many fractions of its length, as well as in its entirety.

Phrase—a small section of a melody having a musical meaning. It signifies about the same as a phrase in written language.

Polyphony—literally, many sounds; refers to music of more than one independent melodic line, or voice. Music for a string quartet, for instance, is polyphonic, and the opposite of monophonic. Polyphonic music can be contrapuntal (when each voice is of relatively equal importance, melodically), or homophonic (when the blend of all the voices into a single chord is essential).

Quarter note— ♩ (see whole note).

Range—the distance in pitch from the lowest note to the highest note of a chord, a melody, an instrument or a voice.

Relative major and relative minor—referring to major and minor keys that contain the same sharps or flats in the key signature. The relative minor is located a minor third below its relative major (see Appendix).

Rest—a pause, or silence, in the music.

7   = rest of an eighth note - ♪

ξ   = rest of a quarter note - ♩

‐   = rest of a half note -   ♩

‐   = rest of whole note -   𝕠

Rhythm—the pattern of beats or pulses.

Rallentando—slowing down; same as ritardando.

Ritardando—slowing down; same as rallentando.

Scale—a stepwise series of notes, ascending or descending in pitch, arranged according to a certain order of half-steps and whole steps.

Sequence—in composition, the repetition of a harmonic or melodic pattern, which starts on successively higher or lower pitches.

Sforzando—accented. Is also written as *sf*, or *sfz*.

Sharp—♯; a symbol indicating a note raised in pitch by a half-step; on the piano this means one key to the right. Sharp also denotes inaccurate pitch, higher than it should be: "He is singing too sharp." (see flat).

Simple time—meter such as $\frac{2}{4}$ or $\frac{4}{4}$ in which each subdivision of the main beats in a measure is made in units of two or three, but not both (see compound time).

Slur—a line connecting two or more notes in a single phrase, which should be played smoothly, and not detached. Where there is a text, it also indicates the number of notes to be sung on one syllable.

Staccato—opposite of legato; Italian for "detached"; should be played lightly and as short as possible, not necessarily with accents: ♩ ♩♩

Indicated by dots over the notes.

Staff—five parallel horizontal lines on which music is written; piano music employs two staves, one for the left hand, the other for the right.

Step—the distance or interval between one note and another note two half-steps away; on the piano this distance is two keys, white or black. A step is also called a whole step.

Stepwise—referring to a melody proceeding by intervals of a half-step or whole step.

Syncopated—having an accent or strong pulse on an otherwise weak beat: $\frac{4}{4}$| 1 2 3 4 |

Tempo—speed. Here are some tempo indications:

Adagio—slowly.

Allegretto—moderately lively.

Allegro—lively, fast.

Andante—moving along moderately, slowly.

Andantino—diminutive of andante; confusingly, it sometimes means less slow, sometimes less fast; the character of the piece must help the performer to decide which.

Cantabile—singing, lyrical.

Dolce—sweetly.

Espressivo—expressively.

Con fuoco—with fire.

Giocoso—joyfully.

Grave—seriously, slowly.

Grazioso—gracefully.

Langsam—slowly.

Largo—broadly, slowly.

Leggiero—lightly.

Lento—very slowly.

Mässig—moderately.

Moderato—moderately.

Mosso—motion; più mosso, faster; meno mosso, slower.

Presto—very fast.

Schnell—fast.

Vivace—lively.

Ternary—three-part.

Texture—referring to the thickness or density—or lightness or thinness—of the musical fabric.

Through composed—music, especially songs, in which there is no repetition of music from phrase to phrase, or verse to verse. The opposite is strophic, in which each verse, or strophe, of a song is set to the same music.

Tie—the connecting line joining two adjacent notes of the same pitch, indicating that the second note should receive no new attack. The same line connecting two notes of different pitch indicates that the notes are to be performed in as smooth, or legato (tied) a way as possible (see slur).

Timbre—the color of a sound, depending on the instrumental vocal combinations used, and caused by the overtones present (see color).

Time signature—the indication, at the beginning of a piece of music, of the meter in which the piece is to be played. It consists of a lower numeral showing how each regular beat will be counted, and an upper numeral showing the number of such beats in the measure: $\frac{2}{4} \frac{3}{4} \frac{4}{4} \frac{6}{8} \frac{9}{8} \frac{3}{2}$

Tonic—the note (or chord based on that note) that gives a scale, or key, its letter name.

Treble—referring to music for high voices or instruments. The treble clef, (𝄞) or G-clef, appears on the five-line staff used by high instruments; it also serves for music played by the right hand at the piano.

Triad—a chord of three notes in which the outer two are an interval of a fifth apart and the middle one is a third from the lowest note. The triad retains its identity even when the notes are played in different positions, called inversions:

C-major triad

Trill—a fast alternating of one note with its upper neighbor. Unless otherwise specified, this upper neighbor is the nearest note that is still in the key signature:

Written   Played   Written   Played

Twelve-tone—the twelve notes that are available in western music, between two notes one octave apart. On the piano there are twelve black and white keys within the octave. Twelve-tone also refers to a style of composition (twelve-tone system) first codified by Arnold Schönberg in 1923-24, in which the twelve notes are arranged in a nonrepetitive order and used as the basic harmonic and melodic structure of a composition.

Upbeat—the pulse before the main beat at the beginning of a measure. It is called "up" probably because of the absence of weight, or because a conductor raises his baton (see downbeat).

Vibrating medium—the material which, when activated, produces sound, such as a string, column of air or membrane.

Whole note—a note, written ○ that receives four counts. The whole note equals two half-notes ♩♩; four quarter-notes ♩♩♩♩; eight eighth-notes ♫♫♫♫ ♫♫♫♫; sixteen sixteenth-notes ♬♬♬♬ ♬♬♬♬ ♬♬♬♬ ♬♬♬♬; etc.

BIBLIOGRAPHY

BOOKS ABOUT THE PIANO

Loesser, Arthur, *Men, Women, and Pianos,* Simon and Schuster, New York. A history of the development of the piano as a musical instrument and social force. Delightfully written by a most witty, well-informed and thoughtful observer.

Schonberg, Harold, *The Great Pianists (from Mozart to the Present),* Simon and Schuster, New York. Written by the distinguished and thorough critic of *The New York Times,* this volume provides interesting facts and stimulating insights into the lives and professional careers of the most powerful performers of the past two hundred years.

Yates, Peter, *An Amateur at the Keyboard,* Random House (Pantheon Books), New York. A good description of the history of keyboard music, of piano construction and of playing techniques, by an author whose curiosity has led him deeper and deeper into a subject he loves.

DICTIONARIES AND ENCYCLOPEDIAS

Apel, Willi, *The Harvard Dictionary of Music,* 2nd ed., Harvard University Press, Cambridge, Mass. Thorough, complete and accurate.

Baker's Biographical Dictionary of Musicians, revised by Nicolas Slonimsky, fifth edition, G. Schirmer, New York. Brief paragraph sketches of the lives of composers and performers of almost every rank.

Cross, Milton, and Ewen, David, *Encyclopedia of the Great Composers and their Music,* Doubleday & Company, Garden City, N.Y. A page or two about each of the best-known composers, and two or three paragraphs about their best-known works.

Illing, R., *A Dictionary of Music,* Penguin Books, London. Brief and concise. Contains two or three lines of data on many composers.

Lloyd, Norman, *The Golden Encyclopedia of Music,* Golden Press, New York. Generously illustrated and popularly written narratives of musicians, instruments, concert halls, musical terminology, etc.

Scholes, Percy A., *The Oxford Companion to Music,* Oxford University Press, ninth ed., London. Rambling and entertaining, with many photographs of composers and musical memorabilia. Good also for definitions of musical terms.

Bernstein, Leonard, *The Joy of Music*, Simon and Schuster, New York. Thoughts on music and the world at large by one of the most famous musicians of our time.

Bernstein, Leonard, *The Infinite Variety of Music*, Simon and Schuster, New York. More deeply pondered ideas about music and where we may be taking it these days.

Cage, John, *Silence*, Massachusetts Institute of Technology, Cambridge, Mass. A varied collection of questions and answers—some deft and defiant, some just daft—but all stimulating and all for real. This contemporary thought maker and music builder takes nothing about music for granted. Note the title, for example.

Copland, Aaron, *What to Listen for in Music*, Mentor (New American Library), New York. One of the best-known American composers reveals what he hears in music.

Copland, Aaron, *Music and Imagination*, Mentor Books, New York. This version of the Charles Eliot Norton Lectures at Harvard University in 1951-52 offers Copland's best guess about where music really originates.

Einstein, Alfred, *A Short History of Music*, Vintage Books, New York. A broad view of the major periods in music history. Less than 200 pages.

Pleasant, Henry, *The Agony of Modern Music*, Simon and Schuster, New York. Examining what he regards as the breakdown of melody, rhythm and harmony, the author concludes that the "music" of the last fifty or sixty years is neither modern nor music.

Sachs, Curt, *The History of Musical Instruments*, W. W. Norton and Co., New York. Complete and beautifully illustrated.

Salzman, Eric, *Twentieth Century Music: An Introduction*, Prentice-Hall History of Music Series, Prentice-Hall, Englewood Cliffs, New Jersey. A careful, factual, not too technical perspective of the musical directions in this century. Other books in this series cover earlier history.

Slonimsky, Nicolas, *Lexicon of Musical Invective*, Coleman-Ross Co., Inc., New York. A startling collection, these writings of critics bitterly condemned the first performances of the best-known works of over forty composers who are admired today.

Stravinsky, Igor, *Poetics of Music*, Vintage Books, New York. The composer's considered and thoughtful opinions on the meaning of music. (For his more acid comments on the musical and antimusical scene, see his several volumes of conversations with Robert Craft.)

Woodworth, G. Wallace, *The World of Music*, Harvard University Press, Cambridge, Mass. The beloved Harvard professor of music and former conductor of the Harvard Glee Club and Radcliffe Choral Society has guided more places and people to more music than anyone will ever know. Here are his urgent thoughts, put together for the Lowell Lectures in Boston, on how music could be nurtured and brought to the hearts of all.

MUSIC FOR FURTHER EXPLORATION

Bach, J. S., *Two-Part Inventions*. Good introduction to gaining in-dependence of the hands. *Anna Magdalena Song Book*. Short pieces in all forms, including songs, especially composed for beginners. *Album of Twenty-One Favorite Pieces for the Piano*, G. Schirmer's Library of Musical Classics, New York City.

Bartók, Béla, *Bartók For Children*. 85 piano pieces without octaves for beginners. Based on Hungarian and Slavonic folk songs. In two volumes (with texts). G. Schirmer's Library of Musical Classics, New York City. *Mikrokosmos*. 153 pieces for piano arranged in progressively difficult order in 7 volumes.

Chopin, Frédéric, *Preludes*. Many of these are too hard for beginners, but some—e.g., Nos. 2, 6 and 15—are slow enough to be mastered.

Mozart, Wolfgang Amadeus. Many collections of early dances, rondos and smaller sonata movements that will give great pleasure.

Scarlatti, Domenico, *Sonatas*. Scarlatti wrote more than 600 of them. Leaf through some of the many collections and pick out those you can handle. They are all very expressive and crystal-clear.

COLLECTIONS

American Composers of Today, Marks Music Corporation, New York. Twenty-three piano pieces introduce the music of contemporary American composers.

Bach, Beethoven and Brahms, edited by Maxwell Eckstein, Amsco Music Publishing Co., New York. Ten or 15 generally short pieces by each composer, some quite easy, some harder, all enjoyable.

Classical Album for Piano, Four Hands, G. Schirmer's Library of Musical Classics, New York. Dances, sonata movements, etc. by Clementi, Beethoven, Haydn, Mozart, Kuhlau, Weber.

Fröhlicher Beethoven (Jolly Beethoven), Fifteen Little Dances for Piano Duet, edited by Leopold J. Beer, Universal Edition No. 11115, New York and Vienna.

Music for Four Hands. Each of these pieces for two people at one piano contains one part written in considerably easier manner than the other. Ensemble playing is excellent for learning to keep good time.

Ravel, Maurice, *Mother Goose Suite*, Durand and Co., Paris. Five pieces for children, especially written for piano duet and later orchestrated. Ravel's piano writing is delicate and beautifully colored.

Stravinsky, Igor, *Five Easy Pieces for Piano Duet*, edited by Gerard Alphenaar, Omega, New York. Easy but exciting music.

The Piano and its Ancestors, Felix Guenther, Editor, Associated Music Publishers, Inc., New York. Music written for clavichord, virginal, harpsichord and the piano by such composers as Bach, Handel, Scheidt, John Bull, Giles Farnaby, Couperin, Rameau, etc. These represent 200 years of music in four countries.

FOR SINGING AND PLAYING

The Fireside Book of Children's Songs, edited by Marie Winn, illustrations by John Alcorn, musical settings by Allan Miller, Simon and Schuster, New York. Favorites, old and new, especially for "Basic Pianists."

The Fireside Book of Folk Songs, selected and edited by Margaret Bradford Boni, arranged for the piano by Norman Lloyd, illustrated by Alice and Martin Provensen, Simon and Schuster, New York. The grandaddy of all song books. Excellently prepared and great fun.

The Harvard University Hymn Book, Harvard University Press, Cambridge, Mass. All the hymns there are, with good texts and in singable keys. Good practice for playing with singers, and for playing four equally balanced musical lines.